The Africa Rising Discourse

Over the last 25 years, the "Africa Rising" discourse has been used to signify hope and promise for the continent, marking a break from previous pessimistic portrayals. This book critically examines that discourse, analyzing recurring themes, tropes, metaphors and imagery.

It traces the evolution of the "Africa Rising" discourse and its connection with Afro-pessimism, providing valuable insights into how the continent is represented and understood. The book explores the tensions, contradictions and impacts of labeling Africa as "rising". Focusing on both local and global social actors, as well as geopolitical influences, it examines how these forces have shaped the discourse over time. Additionally, it highlights how African actors have engaged with and modified the discourse. For instance, the book assesses how in recent years digital media platforms have offered spaces for counternarratives that challenge stereotypical representations, leading to a more nuanced and diverse understanding of Africa's rise.

This book offers valuable insights for researchers in Media and Communication Studies, Digital Media, Journalism, African Studies and Global Studies.

Tracy Tinga is an Assistant Professor in the Department of Media and Communication Studies at the University of Maryland, USA. She holds a PhD in Media and Communication from Temple University's Lew Klein College of Media & Communication. Her research focuses on media and globalization, environmental communication, popular culture and communication for development and social change.

Routledge Contemporary Africa

African Constructions of China
Insights from Ghana and Kenya
Kwaku Opoku Dankwah

African Women and Intellectual Leadership
Life Stories from Western Kenya
Edited by Dannica Fleuss, Maurice N. Amutabi, Emily Achieng' Akuno and Humphrey J. Ojwang

Monuments and Memory in Africa
Reflections on Coloniality and Decoloniality
Edited by John Sodiq Sanni and Madalitso Phiri

Higher Education Transformation in Africa
A Quest for Epistemological Rupture
Edited by Emnet Tadesse Woldegiorgis, Logan Govender and Dennis Zami Atibuni

African Media and Communication
Foundational Conversations
Edited by viola c. milton and Winston Mano

Marriage in Contemporary Zimbabwe
Identity, Community, and Change
Edited by Manase Kudzai Chiweshe

African Fans of European Football
Cultural Globalisation in Kenya and Zimbabwe
Edited by Manase Kudzai Chiweshe and Solomon Waliaula

Legalization of Human Rights in Africa
The Institutionalization of Laws Prohibiting State-Sanctioned Violence and Torture
Edited by Stacey Mitchell, Veraline Nchotu and Lem Lilian Atanga

The Africa Rising Discourse
Tropes, Trophies and Social Actors
Tracy Tinga

For more information about this series, please visit: https://www.routledge.com/Routledge-Contemporary-Africa/book-series/RCAFR

The Africa Rising Discourse

Tropes, Trophies and Social Actors

Tracy Tinga

LONDON AND NEW YORK

First published 2025
by Routledge
4 Park Square, Milton Park, Abingdon, Oxon OX14 4RN

and by Routledge
605 Third Avenue, New York, NY 10158

Routledge is an imprint of the Taylor & Francis Group, an informa business

British Library Cataloguing-in-Publication Data
A catalogue record for this book is available from the British Library

Library of Congress Cataloging-in-Publication Data
Names: Tinga, Tracy, author.
Title: The Africa rising discourse: tropes, trophies & social actors/Tracy Tinga.
Other titles: Tropes, trophies & social actors
Description: Abingdon, Oxon; New York, NY: Routledge, 2025. |
Series: Routledge contemporary Africa |
Includes bibliographical references and index.
Identifiers: LCCN 2024050386 (print) |
LCCN 2024050387 (ebook) | ISBN 9781032750385 (hbk) |
ISBN 9781032750446 (pbk) | ISBN 9781003472124 (ebk)
Subjects: LCSH: Africa–History–1960- | Afrocentrism. |
Afropessimism (Philosophy) | Africa–Relations. |
Africa–In mass media. | Neoliberalism–Africa.
Classification: LCC DT30.5 .T56 2025 (print) |
LCC DT30.5 (ebook) | DDC 960–dc23/eng/20250106
LC record available at https://lccn.loc.gov/2024050386
LC ebook record available at https://lccn.loc.gov/2024050387

ISBN: 978-1-032-75038-5 (hbk)
ISBN: 978-1-032-75044-6 (pbk)
ISBN: 978-1-003-47212-4 (ebk)

DOI: 10.4324/9781003472124

Typeset in Sabon
by Deanta Global Publishing Services, Chennai, India

In loving memory of Rebecca Ng'endo Kamiti.

Mum, you might not have read this, but I know you would have proudly told everyone about it.

Contents

Acknowledgments

I extend my deepest gratitude to Fan Yang my colleague in the Media and Communication Studies Department (University of Maryland Baltimore County) for her guidance and patience throughout the revision process of this project. I also thank my colleague, Jason Loviglio, for his valuable feedback through various drafts of this project. I am equally thankful to my colleagues Elizabeth Patton, Donald Snyder, Kristen Anchor and Bill Shewbridge for their support as I worked on this project.

I am profoundly grateful to my academic advisor, Dr Patrick Murphy (Temple University), for his guidance, kindness and encouragement from the very beginning of this research project. My sincere thanks also go to Dr Fabienne Darling-Wolf (Temple University) and Dr Brian Creech (Lehigh University) for their invaluable feedback during the dissertation stage and their advice throughout my graduate school journey. I couldn't have wished for a more supportive committee! I also thank Dr Herman Wasserman (University of Cape Town) for serving as my external reader and Eminent Scholar Mentor, providing insightful contributions to this project.

To my research participants, who, despite their busy schedules, saw value in this project and generously shared their time and insights, I am truly grateful.

Finally, to my siblings Kui, Ciku, Muya, the rest of the family and friends, who have supported me throughout this journey. I am especially grateful to them for being there for me as I worked on this project while grappling with the loss of mum – thank you! A very special thank you to Cinnamon and Coconut my dogs who faithfully kept me company and encouraged me to take breaks with walks as I worked on every draft!

1 "Another Africa Is Rising: An Africa That Works"

Shifting Representations of the African Continent

On March 30, 1998, *Time* magazine carried a cover story with the title "Africa Rising after decades of famine and war, life is finally looking up for many Africans. Here's why" (McGeary & Michaels, 1998). This cover story presented a stark break from the established pessimistic discourse of the African continent as a place of peril and doom, produced and reproduced by various global media institutions. Indeed, as indicated by earlier editions of the magazine that delivered tales of backwardness and misery on the African continent (Morrow, n.d., September 7; Smith, 1984, January 16), this new, more celebratory presentation of Africa was noteworthy. The idea of "Africa Rising", which signifies hope and promise for the continent, was later picked up by other media entities situated in Western countries (the United States and United Kingdom) such as *The Economist*, *The New York Times*, *The Wall Street Journal* and *The Guardian*. In the decade following its first appearance on *Time*'s cover, it gained traction as the news sources began to and others dedicate increasing amounts of space and visibility to the idea. Over the past 20 years, while the discourse of a continent that is in peril still circulates, this emergent rendering of Africa Rising continues to resonate, reflecting Africa's changing socioeconomic and political landscape. But what do institutions mean when they present Africa as "rising", and why has this discourse gained traction among various transnational institutions?

Critically examining the "Africa Rising" discourse, in this book I make five major arguments. First, I argue that to understand the emergence of this discourse, it is important to acknowledge what was going on within the continent and globally that prompted its emergence. By analyzing the conditions that led to the emergence of this discourse, I suggest that the "Africa Rising" has a dialectical relationship to the Afro-pessimism discourse, as demonstrated through such tropes as women and children in representations of Africa in both discourses. Secondly, I argue that while the analysis of the "Africa Rising" discourse has been examined within transnational media institutions, I also turn attention

DOI: 10.4324/9781003472124-1

to Afrocentric digital platforms, which are online sites that have come up in the last decade with the goal of challenging stereotypical representations of the continent. Drawing on interviews with producers and contributors of some of these platforms, this book shows both that positive attitude and ambivalence exist toward the rising discourse within these platforms. It also shows how the rising discourse is perpetuated explicitly and implicitly within these platforms and how it has been normalized within the continent, making it less obvious to some of its proponents. Thirdly, I argue that while this discourse falls into the trap of homogenizing the continent, a closer look at news and other reports shows a pattern of specific African countries that are labeled as rising mainly because of how well they implement neoliberal policies. This also means that countries named as rising have also lost this status because they did not follow the rubric of neoliberal policies completely. Fourth, discourses are articulated through social actors. I posit that the social actors within the Africa Rising discourse such as governments in African countries, transnational media and China among others are both agents and subjects of this discourse because their actions both promote the rising discourse and are informed by it. Finally, I conclude that the "Africa Rising" discourse is more complex than it has been depicted. It consists of tensions, contradictions and absences that demonstrate how challenging it is to represent an entire continent with just one discourse. More importantly the rising discourse is exemplifying how global neoliberal politics and South–South relations continue to play out within the continent.

This book uses a multi-sited discourse analysis approach which looks at the various sites where the Africa Rising discourse is articulated. This is important because previous studies on this discourse have focused on Western media institutions. As this book demonstrates, the Africa Rising discourse has also been articulated within other institutions that have interests on the continent. These other institutions include international development and humanitarian organizations such as the United Nations, international financial organizations such as the World Bank and transnational corporations such as Goldman Sachs. Here, I focus on the reports that have been produced by these institutions that promote the notion that Africa is rising. By analyzing these reports, I show the influence these institutions have in constructing knowledge about Africa while also demonstrating how these institutions are agents of neoliberal globalization on the continent. As noted, previous scholarship on the Africa Rising discourse has focused on how media institutions in the West have articulated this discourse. This study adds to this by also focusing on how players in the Global South are both subjects and agents of the Africa Rising discourse. This book thus also discusses how the entry of China into African countries as an instance of South–South relations has become an important aspect of the Africa Rising discourse that the institutions use to signify the rise of the continent.

Additionally, this book also discusses how the growth of digital technology in African countries is another signifier of the rising discourse, providing the opportunity for Africa and its diaspora to engage with this discourse. This demonstrates that the Africa Rising discourse is not just a Eurocentric discourse used to promote neoliberal values on the continent, it also shows how people living in various parts of the continent and its diaspora have adopted this discourse to promote Afrocentricity. To reveal how Afrocentricity is promoted through the rising discourse, this book examines various digital platforms that have mushroomed with followers on the continent and its diaspora, looking at how they explicitly or implicitly engage with the rising discourse in the media they produce. To further understand the complexity of engaging with the rising discourse, I conducted interviews with some of the founders, editors and contributors of some of the popular platforms such as *Africasacountry*, *ThisisAfrica* and *Africansontherise* among others.

Criticism on the Africa Rising discourse has pointed out how the Africa Rising discourse like the Afro-pessimism discourse treats the continent like a monolithic place. While this is true, this argument however conceals the complex nature of this discourse. In this book I argue that the rising discourse is not fixed, rather its fluid nature has it shifting between the pessimistic and rising discourse. This temporality can also be observed within the rising discourse as the nations on the continent considered rising keeps changing depending on who is speaking about the rise of the continent. This book also looks closely at which nations on the continent are rising and why. In doing so, this also demonstrates the temporal nature of the rising status and how it shifts from time to time with nations once considered rising, losing this status and other nations gaining it. This is particularly important for understanding which countries within the continent are considered "progressive", which in turn shapes how the rising discourse is articulated. It shows how the rising status is strongly tied to how well nations on the continent adopt neoliberalism. It also shows the power that institutions wield in dictating who is rising on the continent and who isn't. Finally, this book wraps the analysis of the discourse of Africa as rising by discussing some of the tensions and contradictions within the discourse and offering final thoughts on how therefore we should think about the role of African countries in globalization.

Shifting Representations of the African Continent

I use the term "shifting" not to imply that the representations of the African continent have completely changed from pessimistic to optimistic, rather, they are fluid and keep moving from pessimistic to optimistic depending on who is speaking and on various socioeconomic and political circumstances at given times. I also use the term Africa in this book with an understanding that while it is not a homogenous entity, Anglo-American media entities have put forth the notion that Africa is a homogenous albeit amorphous whole. This is highly problematic because the deployment of this rendering of Africa erases the histories and diversities present in the 54 countries in the second largest continent in the world. As such, it is critical to consider why some countries within Africa are given "rising" status while others aren't. This comparative focus is particularly important for understanding which countries within the continent are understood to be experiencing "progress" and thus used as identifiers to shape how the rising discourse is articulated. Additionally, the term "West" is used in this book with the understanding that different Western nations have different relationships with African countries that reveal different discourses ranging from colonialism and imperialism to neoliberalism. Critical scholarship on media representations of African countries by transnational media institutions based in the United States and United Kingdom concludes that coverage toward these countries has been pessimistic (Coombes, 1997; Hawk, 1992; Mayer, 2002; Mengara, 2001; Nothias, 2012; Yrjola, 2011). Scott (2017) and Nothias (2018), however, depart from these conclusions, arguing that there is no empirical basis that Western coverage of African countries is indeed pessimistic. Scott (2017) conducted a meta-analysis of published studies that concluded that US and UK media coverage of Africa was not Afro-pessimistic, arguing that the data collected for previous studies does not warrant the generalizable claims. Scott (2017) also pointed out that none of the previous studies discussed coverage about "Africa Rising". It is, therefore, important to critically analyze coverage on Africa Rising, to understand its meanings, how it relates to Afro-pessimism and what prompts its emergence in Anglo-American news media institutions. As later shown in this chapter and throughout the book, the rising discourse does not dispel the pessimism discourse. In fact, these two dialectic discourses are intertwined, relying on each other to justify the claims they make about Africa.

In response to Scott's (2017) critique of the lack of empirical evidence by studies on representations on Africa, Nothias (2018) conducted a textual analysis of news coverage in British and French press focusing on the 50th independence anniversaries of 24 African countries between 2005 and 2012, concluding that the tropes and language used to represent the continent as tribal, dark, voiceless and homogenous were not as prevalent as critical scholarship suggests. These studies bring up two important questions. First, what has changed about African countries in their 50th year independence that has seen news coverage depart from the Afro-pessimistic discourse, and secondly, what has taken the place of the Afro-pessimistic discourse? This chapter addresses these questions by looking at global transitions and restructuring that have taken place within and outside the continent, their influence on how Anglo-American media represent the continent and the changes that have been taking place in the past 20 years.

"Africa Rising" as a Signifier

Scott (2017) and Nothias (2018)'s conclusions of a more optimist stance toward the African continent reflect broader sociopolitical and economic dynamics that have been at play since the 1990s, influencing how African countries are covered in media institutions based in Western countries and emerging Afrocentric digital platforms. The crux of these dynamics is the implementation of neoliberal economic reforms setting the context for the emergence of the "Africa Rising" discourse. But what exactly does Africa Rising mean? The term "Africa Rising" is characterized by a set of stories and reports that began emerging in the 1990s to date in a variety of media institutions, international financial organizations, and business and development organizations discussed in later sections. This term is mainly used to allude to the economic development or growth of certain countries on the African continent based on their adoption of neoliberal economic and political reforms, as a way of ushering them into the global economy. In other words, while Afro-pessimism was used to justify colonialism and imperialism on the African continent, "Africa Rising" is used to justify contemporary processes of neoliberal globalization. I further tease out the relationship between the rising discourse and neoliberal reform in later sections of this chapter and book. While some of these stories and reports specifically use the term "Africa Rising", others allude to this notion of "growth" by using other related terms such as "emerging", "aspiring", "hopeful", "booming", "development", as well as "growth". Apart from rising economically, Africa Rising within Afrocentric digital platforms also carries an additional connotation of the continent speaking back after centuries of being spoken for. While some Afrocentric digital platforms' editors, producers and content creators are ambivalent of the term Africa Rising, which I discuss in Chapter 3, some also interpret it as Africans finally having the agency to chart their destiny, tell their own stories and showcase their cultures through digital media, hence Africa Rising. All these meanings conveyed by this term and its synonyms, captured through various stories and reports, begin to form a new albeit complex "regime of representation" (Hall, 1997) about the continent, mediating contemporary understanding of the value of Africa for various local, regional and global social actors in the past 20 years and moving forward.

This book considers "Africa Rising" as a "regime of representation" that has been used by various social actors such as local and global media institutions, international development and financial organizations, business organizations and Africans in various parts of the continent and its diaspora, to persuade and influence perceptions and understandings about the continent in the past 20 years. Here, the idea of "articulation" (Grossberg, 1986) is relevant in unpacking how "Africa Rising" functions as a "regime of representation" in these various contexts, at different times, by various social actors. Articulation allows one to observe how different elements that are otherwise not connected become linked up in discourse, paying attention to the conditions under which these elements connect (Grossberg, 1986). In other words, how do various terms, symbols, metaphors, social actors and discourses cohere to the "Africa Rising" discourse and how do they get articulated within this discourse?

Emerging Scholarship on Africa Rising

While this notion of Africa Rising has been present in the public sphere for the past 20 years or so, it is only more recently that scholars have begun paying attention to it. Nothias (2014) focuses on news articles in British, French and American publications on Africa Rising, between 2011 and 2013, concluding that these representations function within dominant discourses of the continent. Flamenbaum (2017) in Bunce, Franks and Paterson (2016) focuses on how young Ghanaians are engaging with the Africa Rising discourse through the New Ghana site, finding that this site continues to reinscribe the dominant discourse about Ghana and Africa at large. Bunce, Franks and Paterson (2016) also bring together various scholars who examine the media image of Africa through various angles such as the framing of Africa in international media coverage in more recent years, humanitarian and development representations, and the political consequences of these representations. Gabay (2018) argues that the Africa Rising discourse emerges following the 2007–8 financial crash, arguing that the rising discourse is seemingly "based at least in part, on anxieties about sustenance of Western economic, political and social models – all of which cohere around practices historically associated with socio-economically privileged people who have been phenotypically white" (p. 211). In other words, "post-crash idealisations of Africa's rise saw in the continent's supposed rise, a validation and a hope for the perpetuation of a mythologised White past, specifically in the emergence of an African homo economicus" (Gabay, 2018, p. 212).

I draw on these scholars as the launching pad for understanding more concretely the work that the rising discourse does, not only within media institutions but also within international development and financial institutions and on Afrocentric digital platforms, by tracing the trajectory of this discourse in these institutions in the past 20 years and linking it to various other discourses that inform how African countries are understood today.

"Africa Rising" within Postcolonial, Development and South–South Frameworks

This book draws on a Postcolonial framework and scholarship on international development, globalization, neoliberal, South–South relations and African studies to understand the emergence of the Africa ising discourse in relation to the history of Afro-pessimism in an intense period of globalization. A postcolonial framework traces the historical trajectory of the representation of the African continent by foreign media, challenging the discourses of backwardness. It also shows the significance of representational practices and the power they hold on the subjects being represented and the role these practices have played in sustaining power structures (Hall, 1997) that perpetuate global inequality. Postcolonial framework also informs the examination of how agents in the Global South attempt to challenge and redefine the discourses about them from the West, as I explore how media producers and consumers on the continent attempt to formulate alternative discourses. Moreover, a postcolonial framework also allows for the interrogation of contradictions and silences within alternative discourses under the rubric of "Africa Rising". Examining the representational practices and their power that has cast the continent in particular ways is important as it links these practices to transnational media and other institutional apparatuses and their interests. The power and influence of these media institutions have undergone significant criticism, as reflected through the Pan-African movement, which aimed to unify people of African descent. This can be viewed as an instance of Africa Rising. Part of the agenda of the Pan-African movement was to help with decolonization and the economic development of African countries. Another event that can also be linked as a precursor to the Africa Rising discourse is the New World Information and Communication Order (NWICO) and MacBride report in the 1980s that revealed the inequalities in global media flows with Anglo-American countries dominating these flows. Apart from NWICO debates, another postcolonial event originating from the continent is the African Renaissance speech delivered by South Africa's President Thabo Mbeki in 1998. This speech presented President Mbeki's vision for the unification and transformation of the continent into a cultural, political and economic powerhouse. These events in a postcolonial Africa can be viewed as part of the discursive constructions of Africa as Rising. In this book, I will engage with the ways the "Africa Rising" discourse especially emerging from the continent is rooted in postcolonialism, while also taking into consideration the emergence of more South–South flows.

Development, neoliberal globalization and translocalization discourses are important as they elaborate the conditions that have led to the emergence of the Africa Rising discourse. They also provide analytical devices for examining how a shift in discourse reveals adjustments in global power relations, guiding assumptions about the ability to act (agency), and in whose interest these adjustments serve. These three discourses are also useful lenses through which to register how shifts in discourse have been influenced by the interplay of power between global and local systems. The Afro-pessimistic discourse was a key element within discourses of development aid in Africa in the 1980s and 1990s. This discourse was central during intensified efforts by donor agencies and countries to help "save" the continent during this period, which led to the creation of an infrastructure, such as the structural adjustment programs, the rise of the non-profit organizations and the adoption of Development Communication strategies to aid in coming up with solutions and effective ways of communicating those solutions in a bid to meet this goal. These development discourses have not been monolithic. In fact, early development programs which were reliant on media-rendered discourses and the subsequent infrastructures that were built to "save" the continent were heavily criticized through the emergence of alternative discourses to development, such as dependency and participatory approaches. This book interrogates the roles that both the dominant and alternative development discourses have played in the formation and circulation of the "Africa Rising" discourse. It is within discourses of development that a pessimistic image of Africa is constructed. It is also within these discourses of development that the image of Africa as rising is also constructed.

Globalization and translocalization discourses are of course also pertinent to the "Africa Rising" discourse, especially with the intensification of China's investments in Africa. This intensification changes the dynamic of global power. Previously, most African countries have relied on European or North American countries with colonial or imperial histories for development aid, this has shifted although not completely to the BRIC countries (Brazil, Russia, India and China) and has seen their foreign policy toward Africa shift to a more strategic one which has seen the increase of bilateral trade agreements, foreign direct investment, infrastructural aid through educational, health and civic projects and peacekeeping missions in different African countries, all in a bid to secure resources for China (Alden, 2005; Wang & Elliot, 2014).

BRIC countries present an interesting dynamic, as they have themselves suffered negative coverage from Anglo-American media constructing them as doomed, which was followed by a shift in discourse to being termed as emerging economies (Zhang, 2010). The rise of the BRIC countries, especially China, has been linked with its influence in other parts of the world, by not only providing infrastructural development but also by extending its "soft power" by broadening its media reach to the African continent (Bailard, 2016; Wasserman, 2016). Even as China advances its influence in African countries, it frames its relationship to African countries as reciprocal, arguing that unlike Africa's relationship with the West, China's relationship is mutually beneficial, based on mutual friendship, goodwill, equality and sharing of knowledge (King, 2013). Through this "reciprocal" relationship, China has been able to secure large tracts of land for farming and oil mines, to be able to feed and fuel its growing population (Cotula, 2009) while investing in infrastructure in these African countries. Given its reciprocal preserves in various African countries, the rise of China can be argued to be linked to the rise of Africa, signifying the rise of the "rest".

The shift in media discourses for BRIC and African countries from doomed to emergent/rising also brings to the fore the role that journalistic practice plays in the production and dissemination of these discourses, and the ways through which these discourses influence not only perceptions of these countries but also the power global media wields in influencing the flow of resources. The production and dissemination of these discourses also signify their value to global media companies as they dedicate even cover stories in some of their flagship magazines and newspapers. This book will therefore also interrogate how the political economy of global media shapes and sustains the production and dissemination of these discourses and the discourses they articulate and what value within a political economic context these discourses may have for these global media entities that circulate them. As noted earlier, there has been a rise of Afrocentric media that have promoted "the rise of Africa" discourse. I also examine the role of Afrocentric digital platforms in constructing alternative discourses about the continent and how they situate their work in relation to the rising discourse.

Multi-sited Discourse Approach and Analytic Framework

This book approaches these questions using a multi-sited critical discourse analysis which goes beyond discourse analysis that looks at the use of language (text and talk) in various sites, paying specific attention to how language connects with the exercise of power. Drawing on Fairclough (1995, p. 1), I seek to expose how communicative acts seen as normal play a role in how one group enacts its power over another. I do so by examining the ways through which discursive practices legitimize control or normalize the social order (Van Dijk, 1993). Critical discourse analysis seeks to expose the discursive practices of injustice by naming them and showing how they get reproduced by everyday practice. It is a resource for people struggling against oppression and domination in its linguistic forms. A critical discourse analysis approach is relevant to this study as it reveals how various institutions exercise power as they deploy the "Africa Rising" discourse, through the texts they produce, how these texts legitimize and normalize this discourse and how this discourse perpetuates marginalization and exclusion within the continent.

The idea of a multi-sited approach is drawn from Marcus (1995) and Hannerz (2003), which goes beyond focusing on a single research site, and instead examining "cultural meanings, objects, and identities in diffuse time-space" (Marcus, 1995, p. 96). This allows for allowing for "connections, associations and putative relationships" (Marcus, 1995, p. 97) to be made across various research sites. In the same way, discourses can occur in various sites at different times for various reasons as is evident with "Africa Rising". A multi-sited discourse analysis explores multiple sites where the Africa Rising discourse has been produced, disseminated and consumed, accounting for the various ways this discourse has been articulated by various institutions at different times from different parts of the world. Apart from examining texts from various institutions, what also makes this study multi-sited is interviewing digital content creators from various platforms that are situated in various parts of the African continent, United States, Europe and Canada. Looking at how these digital content creators from various geographical and digital sites articulate the rising discourse in their work, I trace the translocal linkages that exist between and within the Africa Rising discourse. A multi-sited approach also follows the rising discourse as it moves in different settings, showing its connections and disconnections within various settings because one cannot assume that the rising discourse looks the same in every setting it is articulated.

Having set the theoretical and methodological context for the Africa Rising discourse, the next section begins to unpack the connections this discourse has to the pessimistic discourse, showing how they are both intertwined.

"Africa Does Not Shed Its Stereotypes Easily": Ghosts of Afro-pessimism in the Africa Rising Discourse

Although the Africa Rising discourse departed from the Afro-pessimism discourse with its more hopeful tone of promise for a "new" continent, it heavily relies on Afro-pessimism to make its claim of a "new" and hopeful continent. In other words, the Africa Rising discourse picks up after the Afro-pessimistic discourse. These two ideas have discursively coexisted and relied on each other, functioning as ways of knowing the continent in the global imaginary in the past 20 years. The interconnection of these two discourses is apparent in how they are deployed sometimes explicitly and, at other times, implicitly alongside one another in stories that claim that Africa is rising. These two perspectives are used to affirm each other, with Afro-pessimism used to set the stage for Africa Rising. Africa Rising, therefore, makes sense in that the continent is rising from this history of Afro-pessimism, thus justifying the dominant discourse that indeed the continent was in peril. For instance, the story *Emerging Africa* begins by alluding to Africa's woes by stating,

> AFRICA does not shed its stereotypes easily. Just as it seemed time to drop the old clichés about the continent's corrupt dictators and political chaos, soldiers from America and France have had in the past fortnight to fly into western and central Africa to rescue their nationals from eruptions of violence. At the same time, Africa's need for help seems likely to be one of the chief topics at the annual summit of the Group of Seven rich countries (plus Russia) in Denver next weekend. Out of Africa, it is tempting to conclude, there is never much that is really new.
>
> ("Emerging Africa", 1997)

Here you can see the idea that Africa is emerging is interlaced with the idea of its peril. In another story, the writers point out how countries such as Ghana, Mozambique, Rwanda and Uganda, which were considered as rising, are tainted with a "history of disaster" and "set against the horrors of their quite recent past" ("There is hope; Africa", 2008). This story also compares Ghana to South Korea which were considered to be at par economically in 1957, to 2008 when the story was written, where although Ghana was considered one of the rising countries on the African continent, it was "still some 30 times poorer in wealth per person" compared to South Korea. Similarly, "Africa rising; The hopeful continent" (2011) reminds the reader that although Onitsha market in Southern Nigeria is "also home to millions of highly motivated entrepreneurs and increasingly prosperous consumers", it is also in "a region blighted by corruption, piracy, poverty and disease". McGreary and Michaels (1998) also write that even though hope is rising for people living in various parts of the continent such as Mozambique, Ghana and Mali, hope is a "rare commodity" on the continent because "At the end of the 20th century, we are repeatedly reminded, Africa is a nightmarish world where chaos reigns. Nothing works" (p. 34).

This contrast of a dark and horrific place is used to justify the rise of the continent. To make the idea that Africa is rising conceivable to the audience, the journalists mostly focus on African countries that had a history of calamities and turmoil, to illustrate that things within the continent are changing. In the second chapter, I discuss how various tropes used to represent the Afro-pessimism discourse, later become tropes of the rising discourse as relying on similar tropes, make it easy to argue that countries within the continent are rising. The Africa Rising discourse alludes to Afro-pessimism to illustrate what Africa is rising from and to what. The rising discourse needs a history of failure to warrant its production and circulation as demonstrated by the instances highlighted above. These two forms of discourse are contingent upon one another. Later in the book, I continue to demonstrate the ways that Africa Rising and Afro-pessimism rely on each other by examining how various social actors use the rising discourse and the discourses articulated. Before demonstrating this dialectical relationship between these two discourses, it is important to think about how the Africa Rising became newsworthy to media and other institutions.

"Another Africa Is rising, an Africa That Works": Making "Africa Rising" Sensible

Creech (2015) highlights the importance of examining journalism as a "means of representation", as this enables us to learn how "journalistic objects interface with broader cultural forces and politics" and "cohere as stable objects of journalistic interest" (p. 1012). How then, does "Africa Rising" become an object of journalistic interest, that is, what makes Africa's rise newsworthy to various social actors, and what are the cultural and political forces that constitute it, making it an object of relevance?

In the March 30, 1998, *Time* magazine issue on "Africa Rising", McGreary and Michaels, state "A new spirit of self-reliance is taking root among many Africans as they seize control of their destiny. What are they doing right?". The irony however is that this notion of self-reliance is very much pegged on African countries relying on Western countries and donors. This discourse is a way to show the rest of the world the ways that the African continent has been able to save itself from the doom that was declared upon it by drinking from the well of neoliberalism. The "Africa Rising" discourse began to emerge in Anglo-American media in the 1990s, following a series of events. The most significant of these events was the ushering and implementation of neoliberal policies of development in African countries during this time. This period involved governments yielding their control of various institutions to the markets, through the implementation of structural adjustment programs, the adoption of Western ideals of democracy and the free-market economy.

Neoliberalism, Harvey (2007) postulates, is "a theory of political economic practices proposing that human well-being can best be advanced by the maximization of entrepreneurial freedoms within an institutional framework characterized by private property rights, individual liberty, unencumbered markets and free trade" (p. 22). Similarly, Peet (2002) defines neoliberalism as, a set of beliefs that stem from the ideas of "political democracy, individual freedom and the creative potential of unfettered entrepreneurship" (p. 62), where the role of the government is to provide infrastructure while allowing the markets to flourish without state interference. Neoliberal development policies were, therefore, intended to reengineer the economic landscape of countries, with the hope that this would bolster their standing in the global economy. Neoliberalism arose from the Washington Consensus in the 1990s, which instigated the formation of the World Trade Organization (WTO), an institution that became key in promoting neoliberalist ideals as it "set the standards and rules for interaction in the global economy" (Harvey, 2007, p. 93) that would open up the rest of the world to the flow of capital. Other institutions that played a significant role in endorsing neoliberalist ideals include the World Bank and International Monetary Fund (IMF).

Emeagwali & Kapoor (2011) refers to these "standards and rules" as "conditionalities". Peet and Hartwick (1999) list these conditionalities as, fiscal discipline, where budget deficits would not surpass the GDP by more than 2%, the redirection of public expenditure to education; health and infrastructure; tax reform competitive exchange rates; liberalization of trade, where trade restrictions would be replaced by tariffs; privatization of state-owned enterprises; and deregulation and securing of property rights. Neoliberal development policy, therefore, "came to consist in withdrawing government intervention in favor of the rationalization of an economy through disciplining by the market and by self-interested individuals efficiently choosing between alternatives in the allocation of resources" (Peet & Hartwick, 1999, p. 52). As these processes began taking root in various African countries in the 1990s with varying intensities, and began "transforming" the economies, physical and institutional infrastructures, as the magic pill to underdevelopment, prescribed by International Financial Organizations (IFO), the Africa Rising discourse began to emerge. The adoption of neoliberal policies is heavily alluded to as a factor of Africa's rise. One news story states,

> The efforts of Africans themselves have counted for more. The idea that lasting prosperity demands stable government and the rule of law has taken hold almost everywhere (the coup in Sierra Leone was condemned across the continent). Most African governments, moreover, have adopted promising economic policies: sound money,

> fiscal rectitude and the encouragement of private business are their mantras.
>
> ("Emerging Africa", 1997)

Another story states:

> You might call it a second-chance African revolution. What every country striding forward shows is that progress comes first to those who adopt the principles and practices of capitalist democracy. There are some common lessons here that any African nation can learn: free-market economics works, including privatization, entrepreneurship and often the stern measures of wholesale reform to jump-start failed economies. So does agricultural self-sufficiency, starting from the bottom up. And decentralization, spreading development outside urban capitals to the vast rural majority. And women's empowerment.
>
> (McGreary & Michaels, 1998)

In another report:

> The presumption of state control under the rubric of "African socialism" (an illusory third way) has been junked. Most local leaders accept that Africa must join the global economy to prosper, however shaky it looks right now. The mobile-phone revolution has hugely helped Africans, especially poor peasants and traders. Banking systems are modernizing and mortgages more readily offered to an emerging middle class. Businessmen around the world have been investing more, especially in Africa's better-governed countries. Even those that lack natural wealth have grown a bit faster. The spectacular advent of China into Africa's market is, on balance, a bonus.
>
> ("There is hope Africa", 2008)

These three instances present a snapshot of the amount of weight that the adoption of neoliberal development policies is given in the rise of Africa. All three accounts demonstrate how Africa Rising as a discourse is used to justify neoliberal reform by showing the "transformation" taking place in various countries. This role of neoliberalism is also discussed in Chapter 4, which examines the role of social actors in promoting this discourse and how these social actors serve as "technologies of neoliberalism" within it.

The adoption of neoliberal development policies to lead Africa out of poverty is promoted through a series of events that took place in the 1990s, influencing the emergence of the Africa Rising discourse. One such factor is the Group of 7 (G7) summit in 1997. The June 14, 1997, issue of *The Economist*, titled *Emerging Africa*, states,

> A new sort of African leader is trying to break the addiction to foreign aid, and to the idea that Africa's woes can be blamed forever on the legacy of colonialism. They are beginning to see their countries not as victims but as emerging markets, capable by dint of their own efforts of profiting from the freer flow of trade in the global economy.

This issue was produced in the context of the Group of 7 (G7) summit that took place on June 20–22, 1997, in Denver, Colorado. This summit brought together leaders from the richest developed nations which at the time included the United States, the United Kingdom, France, Germany, Italy, Japan and Canada. Although Russia was represented, it hadn't been recognized as a member at the time. The 1997 Communique of the summit to the press highlighted ten specific challenges in relation to the African continent, that the G7 were committed to address. These are summarized in this statement: "Our objective is not only to facilitate the progressive integration of African countries into the world economy, but also to foster the integration of poor populations into economic, social and political life of their countries" (*Denver Summit of Eight Communique*, 1997).

The production of *The Economist, Emerging Africa* issue was in light of the upcoming summit at the time and relies on the G7 summit to construct the notion that Africa is emerging. The crux of this issue was that the leaders of the G7 summit ought to focus more on the African countries that were adjusting their national policies to allow for their integration into the global economy. The G7 summit, therefore, became symbolic in framing the media coverage about the continent in that specific moment and grants the publication the authority to make the claim that Africa is emerging as seen from the quote below.

> But, thanks mainly to what the Americans are calling their "Africa Initiative", stressing trade rather than aid, the G7 meeting in Denver has a chance to think in a fresh way about the continent. Africa still needs help-and as the countries that dominate the IMF and the World Bank, G7 members are well placed to determine its shape. But the rich world must stop asking "What can we do about Africa?" and ask "How do we respond to those African countries that are making real progress, and encourage others to do likewise?
>
> ("Emerging Africa" 1997)

Another event that is symbolic in relation to the Africa Rising discourse was President Bill Clinton's tour of Africa in March 1998. This trip was symbolic because President Bill Clinton was the first sitting United States president to tour the continent, and it signified interest in building relationships with African countries. It was also significant because it created a new epistemology of the continent by recasting it from a dark, horrific place that is bad for business to a lucrative business hub by showcasing the changes that were taking place in various African countries, which the president was set to tour. The countries that President Clinton toured included Ghana, Rwanda, Uganda, South Africa, Botswana and Senegal. While in Uganda, President Clinton attended the one-day Kampala Summit, meeting with leaders from Congo, Eritrea, Ethiopia, Kenya, Rwanda and Tanzania. As will be discussed later, the specific countries he visited and others mentioned elsewhere are a significant part, and signifiers, of the Africa Rising discourse. It is within the context of this presidential tour that *Time* magazine on March 30, 1998, stated,

> For so long the victim of historical circumstance, Africa is finally a beneficiary. The end of the cold war freed countries from 30-odd years of disastrous involvement in the superpowers' proxy conflicts. Old ideologies crumbled, taking with them the failed socialist methods of Marx and opening the way to capitalist reforms. The demise of apartheid gave the continent a huge psychological – and economic and political – boost. A generation of African leaders who grew up to despise the exploitation of postcolonial dictators and kleptocrats has begun to supplant them. In recognition of all that, Bill Clinton set off last Sunday on the first extensive tour of Africa by a sitting U.S. President. His aim is to cast a high-wattage spotlight on the continent's emerging democracies, economic growth and social progress and to promote a new relationship with the U.S. Of course, the Administration also sees a largely untapped market and wants to encourage American businessmen to get there first. Africans hope Clinton will show them that the U.S. is ready to be a partner instead of patron.
>
> (McGreary & Michaels, 1998)

It was also important that the trip was a precursor to the passing of the Africa Growth and Opportunity Act (AGOA) by the US Congress in 2000. Signed by President Clinton, the act reinforced the message that African countries were worth the investment. According to the Brookings *Africa Growth and Opportunity Act: Looking Back Looking Forward* Report, AGOA "redefined" US relations with Africa from donor-recipient to trade partnership as a catalyst to economic growth and poverty alleviation, as it eliminated duties and tariffs of over 6000 products being imported into the US from beneficiary African countries (Schneidman & Lewis, 2012). AGOA was signed into law in the year 2000 for 15 years and was renewed in 2015 for ten more years. AGOA further mirrored the conditionalities set by the World Bank and International Monetary Fund structural adjustment programs.

These three events, the G7 summit in Denver, Colorado, in 1997, President Bill Clinton's tour to Africa in 1998 and the signing of AGOA into law in 2000 – with an explicit neoliberal agenda for the continent are symbolic as their newsworthiness to transnational media institutions set the tone for the "Africa Rising" discourse.

Having given context for the emergence of the "Africa Rising" discourse, Chapter 2 identifies and traces the deployment of key terms, images, recurring tropes and metaphors used in the depiction of the continent as rising, analyzing how and why they function as tropes discourse. Specifically, this chapter examines how women, youth, children, the middle class, cities, ideologies such as democracy and other metaphors are used as tropes to represent the rise of Africa. Chapter 3 examines how Afrocentric digital platforms which are online sites that have been formed within the last decade, with the goal of challenging stereotypical representations of the continent. This chapter discusses the roles that these platforms play in the representation of the continent and the ways they are influenced and influence the rising discourse. Chapter 4 pays attention to the specific countries that are labeled as rising on the continent. I discuss how the neoliberal rubric used to assign the rising status for countries on the continent is problematic and leads to a game of musical chairs as countries awarded this status lose it as other countries gain it depending on how well they adhere to the rubric of implementing neoliberal policies. This chapter continues to demonstrate how much transnational institutions wield power over the way African countries are known globally, as they decide which African countries are worth noting as rising. Chapter 5 discusses the social actors within the "Africa Rising" discourse and the various roles that they play as they act both as its agents and subjects. The key social actors identified include transnational media, government officials, citizens in various African countries, international financial corporations, transnational corporations and other countries in the Global South. This chapter also discusses the importance of translocalization in shaping the Africa Rising discourse as countries such as China partner with various African countries. Placing this analysis within more current processes of globalization, this chapter considers how the rise of African countries is compared to the rise of other "rising" countries in the Global South. Chapter 6 reflects on the contradictions and absences within this discourse, offering final thoughts on how it is immersed in a web of global power relations. It will also reflect on the complexity of the rising discourse as an alternative way of talking about the continent and the epistemological implications it presents. For instance, the Africa Rising discourse does not dispel the Afro-pessimistic discourse; it in fact reinforces it.

References

Africa rising; The hopeful continent. (2011, December 3). The Economist, 401(8762), 15(US). General OneFile.

Alden, C. (2005). China in Africa. *Survival*, *47*(3), 147–164.

Bailard, C. S. (2016). China in Africa: An Analysis of the Effect of Chinese Media Expansion on African Public Opinion. . *The International Journal of Press/Politics*, *21*(4), 446–471.

Bunce, M., Franks, S., & Paterson, C. (2016). *Africa's media image in the 21st century: From the "heart of darkness" to "Africa rising"*. Routledge.

Coombes, A. E. (1997). *Reinventing Africa: Museums, material culture and popular imagination in late Victorian and Edwardian England.* Yale University Press.

Cotula, L. (2009). *Land grab or development opportunity?: Agricultural investment and international land deals in Africa.* Iied.

Creech, B. (2015). Disciplines of truth: The 'Arab Spring', American journalistic practice, and the production of public knowledge. *Journalism*, *16*(8), 1010–1026.

Denver Summit of the Eight: Communique. (n.d.). Retrieved July 1, 2024, from https://1997–2001.state.gov/issues/economic/summit/communique97.html

Emeagwali, G., & Kapoor, D. (2011). The Neo-Liberal Agenda and the Imf/World Bank Structural Adjustment Programs With Reference To Africa. In *Critical Perspectives on Neoliberal Globalization, Development and Education in Africa and Asia* (pp. 3–13). SensePublishers. https://doi.org/10.1007/978-94-6091-561-1_1

Emerging Africa. (1997, June 12). *The Economist*, *343*(8021).

Fairclough, N. (1995). *Critical discourse analysis: The critical study of language.* Longman.

Flamenbaum, R. (2017). A "New Ghana" in "Rising Africa." *Africa's Media Image in the 21st Century: From the "Heart of Darkness" to "Africa Rising"*, 116–126.

Gabay, C. (2018). *Imagining Africa: Whiteness and the Western Gaze.* Cambridge University Press.

Grossberg, L. (1986). On postmodernism and articulation: An interview with Stuart Hall. *Journal of Communication Inquiry*, *10*(2), 45–60.

Hall, S., & others. (1997). *Representation: Cultural representations and signifying practices* (Vol. 2). Sage.

Hannerz, U. (2003). Being there... And there... And there! Reflections on multi-site ethnography. *Ethnography*, *4*(2), 201–216.

Harvey, D. (2007). Neoliberalism as creative destruction. *The ANNALS of the American Academy of Political and Social Science*, *610*(1), 21–44. https://doi.org/10.1177/0002716206296780

Hawk, B. G. (1992). *Africa's media image.* Praeger Publishers.

King, K. (2013). *China's aid and soft power in Africa: The case of education and training*. Boydell and Brewer.

Marcus, G. E. (1995). Ethnography in/of the world system: The emergence of multi-sited ethnography. *Annual Review of Anthropology*, *24*(1), 95–117.

Mayer, R. (2002). *Artificial Africas: Colonial images in the times of globalization*. UPNE.

Mcgeary, J., & Michaels, M. (1998, March 30). Africa rising. *Time*, *151*(12).

Mengara, D. M. (2001). *Images of Africa: Stereotypes & realities*. Africa World Press.

Morrow, L. (n.d.). Africa: The scramble for survival. *Time*. Retrieved January 17, 2018, from http://content.time.com/time/magazine/article/0,9171,976401,00.html

Nothias, T. (2012). Definition and scope of Afro-pessimism: Mapping the concept and its usefulness for analysing news media coverage of Africa. *Leeds African Studies Bulletin*, *74*, 54–62.

Nothias, T. (2014). 'Rising','hopeful','new': Visualizing Africa in the age of globalization. *Visual Communication*, *13*(3), 323–339.

Nothias, T. (2018). How Western journalists actually write about Africa: Re-assessing the myth of representations of Africa. *Journalism Studies*, *19*(8), 1138–1159.

Peet, R. (2002). Ideology, discourse, and the geography of hegemony: From socialist to neoliberal development in postapartheid South Africa. *Antipode*, *34*(1), 54–84.

Peet, R., & Hartwick, E. R. (1999). *Theories of development*. Guilford Press.

Schneidman, W., & Lewis, Z. A. (2012). *The African growth and opportunity act: Looking back, looking forward*. Citeseer.

Scott, M. (2017). The myth of representations of Africa: A comprehensive scoping review of the literature. *Journalism Studies*, *18*(2), 191–210. https://doi.org/10.1080/1461670X.2015.1044557

Smith, W. E. (1984, January 16). The light that failed; A military coup brings an abrupt end to Nigeria's democratic experiment. *Time*, 123–124.

There is hope; Africa. (2008, October 11). *The Economist*, *389*(8601), 20(US). General OneFile.

Van Dijk, T. A. (1993). Principles of critical discourse analysis. *Discourse & Society*, *4*(2), 249–283.

Wang, F.-L., & Elliot, E. A. (2014). China in Africa: Presence, perceptions and prospects. *Journal of Contemporary China*, *23*(90), 1012–1032. https://doi.org/10.1080/10670564.2014.898888

Wasserman, H. (2016). China's "soft power" and its influence on editorial agendas in South Africa. *Chinese Journal of Communication*, *9*(1), 8–20.

Yrjola, R. (2011). Visual politics and celebrity humanitarianism. *Images in Use: Towards the Critical Analysis of Visual Communication*, *44*, 199.

Zhang, L. (2010). The rise of China: Media perception and implications for international politics. *Journal of Contemporary China*, *19*(64), 233–254.

2 "Lions on the Move"

Symbolic and Discursive Constructions Within the Rising Discourse

The cover page of the March 30, 1998, *Time* magazine "Africa Rising" issue features the image of an African woman, Awa Kone of Mali. In this image, the woman's head is wrapped in a headscarf. She is made to appear simple, she is not adorned in any makeup or jewelry. The headscarf suggests a traditional woman. She stares intently into the camera with no smile on her face. Next to the image of this woman, the words "Africa Rising" are colorfully typed in capital letters, and next to them in small white font, "After decades of famine and war, things are looking up for many Africans, here's why" and the name of the woman in small font. The face of this woman from Mali is made to stand for the rise of the continent. This imagery is part of a cluster of images that are used to visually depict the rise of the continent. Burke (1966) defines "clusters" as "what goes with what" (p. 20) and posits that clusters begin to emerge in the process of communication as communicators rely on certain terms to express specific ideas. It is thus imperative to examine what terms, images and symbols are used in the process of communicating the rise of Africa, that is, "what goes with what" in relation to "Africa Rising". This chapter identifies the key terms, images, recurring tropes and metaphors used in portraying Africa as a rising continent. It compares the tropes, imageries and symbols used to represent Africa in a pessimistic light to those used to depict Africa as rising. This comparison shows how these two discourses about Africa are complex and intertwined. Some of the tropes discussed include women, youth, children and the middle class. Furthermore, the chapter delves into the imagery employed to visually represent the concept of Africa Rising, such as lions, Baobab trees and giraffes. Additionally, the chapter examines the role of various African cities in promoting the rising discourse. It reveals how cities play a crucial role in the processes of globalization and how they are often depicted as hubs of progress and economic development. Lastly, the chapter explores the idea of democracy as one of the key factors representing the rise or fall of African countries. It critically

DOI: 10.4324/9781003472124-2

examines how democracy is portrayed within the discourse and analyzes its implications for understanding the trajectory of African nations.

Women, Youth and Children: Neoliberal Subjects and Neoliberal Agents

Apart from Awa Kone's image on the cover page, the story relies on other images of women working on farms to symbolize a rising continent. There are also images of men at work doing welding and other industry-related work, conveying the idea of construction and rebuilding. Another image is that of a male teacher in a classroom with students. It is interesting to compare the images used to represent a working woman versus a working man. While these images of men are used, their role in economic growth is not as highlighted as that of women. From the story, we learn this about Awa Kone, the woman on the cover page:

> Women have always labored twice as hard as men in Africa, tending house, raising children, harvesting their husbands' fields. When we met Awa Kone, she was watering, bucketful by bucketful, young banana and mango trees and small plots of onions, tomatoes and eggplants. This garden in the tiny 10-family settlement of Tenemakana is a cooperative moneymaker for the village wives. The women pool the profits and then loan out the money to each other at 9% interest. No woman has ever defaulted. When they have earned enough, Kone and her friends plan to build a clinic.
>
> (McGreary & Michaels, 1998)

This focus of women as entrepreneurs is further illustrated in *The Economist*'s March 2, 2013, "A hopeful continent" issue, which had on the cover page the image of an African woman seated in what appears to be a stall in the market, holding two juicy pineapples with a big smile on her face. At the bottom of the cover page are the words "A hopeful continent" printed in bold white text. The image of women in the marketplace as entrepreneurs is used to signify hope for the continent. Similarly, the articles focus on Lucia Qauchey, the president of the Ghana Association of Women Entrepreneurs (McGreary & Michaels, 1998) representing the voice of women entrepreneurs on the continent, which is used to signify growth for the continent.

The role of African women in economic growth and the rise of Africa resonates with discourses about gender and development. Wilkins (2016) states, "Development discourse serves as more than a set of phrases used to explain the world and its myriad problems. This discourse structures the allocation of resources toward particular subjects as well as designated countries and communities" (p.3). The rising discourse focuses its attention on the allocation of resources to women, children and youth from specific African countries such as Ghana, Mozambique and Eritrea. Approaches advocating for the role of women in development and economic growth have evolved from women in development (WID) which critiqued the absence of women or their passive role in development projects (Boserup, 1975), to gender and development (GAD), which recognized the power differences between men and women as a challenge to development (Miller,& Razavi, 1995)), to a neoliberal approach that emphasizes the role of the woman as an entrepreneur (Wilkins, 2016). Wilkins (2016) states, "Building on a neoliberal discourse of development that privileges individuals as central actors in social change, women are conceptualized as actively engaged individuals who participate in free markets as consumers or as small-scale entrepreneurs" (p. 24). This has culminated in the woman, in this case African woman, becoming a trope for the growth on the continent. This new image of Africa is based on the ability of the woman to become an entrepreneur. It departs from the Afro-pessimistic discourse where women and children were mostly portrayed as victims. This set the context for the introduction of micro entrepreneurship projects where small groups of people – in this case women and, as will be discussed later, youth – are offered loans to finance small businesses as a solution to poverty by promoting self-reliance.

This idea is reflected in the story about Awa Kone and her women's group mentioned earlier. The focus on women specifically is justified by the notion that "In the microenterprise scheme, development programs assume, often explicitly, that women are more likely than men to spend their money efficiently, to allocate resources toward family interests, and to repay their loans" (Wilkins, 2016, p. 53). The rising discourse not only represents a shift in how women from the continent have been represented from victims to entrepreneurs, but this shift is also used to represent a triumph of neoliberalism within the continent, albeit uncritically, with women cast as neoliberal agents (entrepreneurs) and subjects (consumers) who are leading the economic boom in various African countries. The discourse on the rise of Africa articulates development discourses by focusing its attention to specific subjects, in this case women, and highlighting their role in the economic growth of the continent.

The images of children are also used as symbols for the rise of the African continent. In 1997 when *The Economist* published the "Emerging Africa" issue, it featured the image of four African children on the cover page against a black background. In this image, we can only see the children's faces and upper body, which are not clothed. The children in this image are not smiling just like Awa Kone mentioned previously. Unlike with the case of Awa Kone, we are not told who the children are and where they are from. Another instance where a child has been used to depict the rise of Africa is in *The Economist*, 2011 "Africa Rising" issue where the magazine used the silhouette of a child flying a rainbow-colored kite shaped like the map of the African continent. Nothias (2014) argues that the rainbow is used to symbolize South Africa, "the rainbow nation" and one of the continent's economic powerhouses. This also reflects how some countries like South Africa are picked to represent the rise of the continent. This is either done implicitly as in this case or explicitly as will be discussed in the chapter on Trophy countries. In this image we just see the silhouette of a child, unlike in the 1997 edition where the actual images of children were used. In 2017 *The Economist* also published a special report on technology in Africa, titled "The Leapfrog Model". The cover page of this edition is the image of four girls in a classroom, wearing headphones and smilingly looking at tablets. This image of four girls also carries with it the symbolic role of girls and women in the rise of the continent as previously discussed. While in the aforementioned stories there isn't a discussion of children, their images are symbolically used to conjure the rise of Africa. When children are mentioned in other rising stories, the focus is on the opportunities that the economic growth enables them to have, such as access to education and healthcare: "But most Africans no longer fear a violent or premature end and can hope to see their children do well" ("A hopeful continent", 2013). Children and women were also used as symbols of the Afro-pessimistic discourse to depict suffering of humanity in catastrophes such as famine, diseases, natural calamities and war among others, as a call to action by emotionally and morally drawing audiences across the world through the "globalization of suffering" (Kleinman & Kleinman, 1996). Within the rising discourse the image of children and women gets transformed into symbols of hope for the continent.

"Africa's Demographic Dividend": Youth as Rising Symbols and the Growing Middle Class

Youth are also used as symbols of the rising discourse. Their significance within the rising discourse, like that of women, is through their contribution to economic growth. This contribution is first through their role in national building through national service. In the Africa Rising edition of *Time* magazine in 1998, Eritrea is identified as one of the countries that is rising with one of the factors credited for this being the contribution of young people through their national service, where some serve in the army and others work on infrastructure-based construction projects: "Up here, some are also planting trees to revive the blighted landscape. 'I like doing it', says 24-year-old Daniel. 'I teach people how to do things, and that is a way to develop our country fast'" (McGreary & Michaels, 1998). Young people also play a role within this rising discourse through their capacity as entrepreneurs and consumers.

> Population trends could enhance these promising developments. A bulge of better-educated young people of working age is entering the job market and birth rates are beginning to decline. As the proportion of working-age people to dependents rises, growth should get a boost. Asia enjoyed such a "demographic dividend", which began three decades ago and is now tailing off. In Africa it is just starting.
>
> ("*The hopeful continent*", 2011)

Africa's demographic dividend is also expressed through institutional and business reports highlighting the rise of the continent. The next chapter looks more closely at the role of business and development reports in the production of this discourse. These reports also use the youth population within the African continent to discuss its ability to rise, noting that by the year 2040 the continent will have 1.1 billion people of working age (Roxburgh et al., 2010; Bughin, 2016).

"The Consuming Class Is Attracting Western Shopkeepers": The Middle Class as a Trope

The rise of Africa is also predicated on the rising middle class on the continent ("*The new champions*", 2008; "*Africa Rising: The hopeful continent*", 2011; "*The gateway to Africa*", 2012; "*Doing it my way*", 2013; "*Making Africa work*", 2016; Wonacott, 2011)

> There's a new gold rush under way for the African consumer, a campaign that spans the continent and aims to reach an emerging middle class. These are the people who have begun to embrace cellphone messages, restaurant meals and trips down supermarket aisles.
>
> (Wonacott, 2011 p. B1)

The growing middle class in various countries on the continent as a trope for the rise of the continent reflects Lerner's (1958) parable of the chief and the grocer, with the grocer able to progress in society by embracing modernity unlike the chief. Similarly, the middle class and their desire for modernity or modern things are like the grocer. Like the grocer, middle class is identified by what they consume as indicated in the quote below.

> Chima Odu, 32 years old Lagos, Nigeria undergraduate degree in biochemistry Works in human resources for foreign oil company, makes about $50,000 a year Married, with one-year-old child and a baby on the way Owns home often travels to oil hub Port Harcourt, to see parents Says he can't resist buying new products and clothes and that younger middle- and upper-class Nigerians are eager to be seen with the latest gadgets. "It's what's in vogue," he says. "I mean, why would I walk in here to buy a new phone if I have one phone already? I'm a shopaholic."
>
> (Wonacott, 2011 p. B1)

Connors (2011) discusses the growing market for pre-owned cars from the United States as a status symbol for upward mobility among Nigerians. Lerner (1958) posited that modernity for developing nations would be accessed through the construction of physical infrastructure such as roads, linking villages to cities and through media, as they allow for physical mobility, the opportunity to travel to new worlds and aspire to change. Owning a car, albeit a preowned one, is used here as a sign of a rising Nigeria and Africa as it gives access to physical mobility. It also signifies the growth of infrastructure in the form of road networks, that make owning a car an attractive venture. The value of the middle class in the context of the rising discourse is in their ability to consume things that allow them to travel to new worlds, aspire to change and hence want to consume more. As a trope for modernity and a rising continent, the middle class and their desire to consume the latest products rebrands the image of Africans from poor and helpless, hence lacking value to investors, to a group that can be profitable to "Western shopkeepers" ("*Doing it my way*", 2013). It rebrands and commodifies the continent as a way of justifying neoliberal intervention.

The middle class on the continent is not only used to symbolize modernity on the continent but just as the lack of Western modernity was used to justify colonialism on the continent, the growing middle class is used to justify the need for the free market, where the desires and tastes of this group can be met. The growing middle class as a trope for a rising continent has more to do with the value that this group offers "Western shopkeepers". The rise of the middle class also coincides with the growth of cities/urbanization. The idea of the middle class and cities is consistent with Western ideas of modernity and modern lifestyles as reflected in the modernization paradigm. The growth of cities is one of the hallmarks of modernization (Lerner, 1958) with the growth of cities in African countries becoming tropes for the rising discourse.

"First-World Infrastructure and Third-World Cost": The Role of Cities in Africa's Rise

Massey (2007) states that "cities are central to neoliberal globalization" and "it is not just that neoliberalism affects cities, but also that cities have become key institutional arenas in and through which neoliberalism is itself evolving" (p. 9). It is therefore not surprising that cities on the African continent have become tropes for the rising discourse. Cities are symbolic of Africa's rise as they not only present the right conditions for neoliberalism to take root, but they are also spaces where you can see neoliberalism in action through their function as production, consumption and distribution centers.

Cities on the African continent such as Johannesburg, South Africa; Lagos, Nigeria; Accra, Ghana; Nairobi, Kenya; Cape Town, South Africa; etc. therefore easily lend themselves to be tropes of the rising discourse, as it is within cities that you can more clearly see the movement of "scapes" (Appadurai, 1990) as they become hubs for production, consumption and distribution. This is made apparent in *The Economist*'s 2013 "*Africa Rising: A hopeful continent*" edition, in which Oliver August travels across 23 countries on the continent and reports about his trip. They state,

> your correspondent travelled overland across the continent from Dakar to Cape Town (see map, previous page), taking in regional centres such as Lagos, Nairobi and Johannesburg as well as plenty of bush and desert. Each part of the trip focused on one of the big themes with which the continent is grappling – political violence, governance, economic development.
>
> (August 2013 p. 3)

This trip itself is quite symbolic as it bares resemblance to historical explorations of the continent leading up to its scramble and partition – only, this time, the scramble is by foreign multinationals. The juxtaposition of "regional centers" against "plenty of bush and desert" makes the role that cities play in the rising discourse more significant, as it is within these regional centers that the correspondent is able to see the consequences of neoliberalism such as the local bustling market places alongside foreign multinationals as described below.

> After an uninterrupted journey through wooded valleys the bus arrives in Conakry. The capital of Guinea sits on a narrow rocky peninsula stretching into the choppy Atlantic. The city is bursting at the seams and the traffic is jammed. Every alley is a retail space. Fishermen hang their catch on strings in the shade. Hilton and Radisson are

> building hotels for investors to stay in. House prices have taken off. International flights are packed, as are berths in the port.
>
> (August 2013 p. 5)

Kristof (2007) in his article "Africa land of hope" celebrates the economic growth on the continent and attributes this to economic reform, stating: "So here's an investment tip: Buy real estate in Benin and Rwanda" (P A13). While he does not mention specific cities in these countries, what he alludes to is the potential for investment. We can see these investments taking place a few years later in cities, as illustrated by Oliver August chronicling his journey across the continent. The rising discourse is an attempt to persuade foreign multinationals of the value of African cities, with some companies beginning to establish headquarters for Sub-Saharan Africa in various African cities. For instance, firms like General Electric, Coca-Cola, Nestle and Heineken have established their Sub-Saharan Africa headquarters in Nairobi, Kenya. South Africa is said to host about 75% of foreign multinationals on the continent (Musau, 2017). In November 2018, BBC established a bureau in Nairobi, Kenya, which has been termed its largest bureau outside the United Kingdom. KPMG, an international auditing firm, launched a report "The role of cities in Africa's Rise" stating:

> Cities in Africa are at the heart of the continent's economic reconfiguration and are an integral part of unlocking its future potential. Cities encapsulate exciting new growth prospects around demography – and the booming, youthful population, urbanisation and the burgeoning middle class, all of which bodes well for consumer spending, investment and a growing labour force. Cities also encourage modernisation, openness and connectedness which are important pre-conditions of sustained economic success.
>
> ("*The role of cities in Africa's Rise*", 2012 p. 6)

As illustrated in the above quote, cities provide the crucible for the agents and subjects of neoliberalism to mix, thus becoming an important trope of the rising discourse. This has prompted a series of reports and articles recognizing cities (Africa's 10 wealthiest cities, 2018; World's largest cities will be in Africa, 2018; McDubus, 2017). More recently, the Global Financial Centers Index (GFCI) 34, published in September 2023, ranks cities such as Casablanca, Morocco, as the leading African financial center. Other financial centers include Mauritius, Kigali, Johannesburg, Nairobi, Cape Town, and Lagos. Additionally, some of these cities such as Lagos, Nairobi and others such as Cairo have also been identified as technology hubs within the continent (Akabor, 2023).

"Being Nicely Democratic": Embracing Democracy as a Hallmark of Africa's Progress

As earlier discussed, democracy through the adoption of multiparty politics and liberalization of the airwaves was a conditionality for countries implementing neoliberal economic reform receiving aid from donor institutions. In fact, McGreary and Michaels (1998) refer to it as "adopting capitalist democracy". Here, it is interesting to see the connection between economic freedom and political freedom, which informs how democracy is used as a yardstick to measure how successful a country was at adopting Western reform and as a trope for the rising discourse. Based on this association of economic and political freedom, democracy as a trope for the rising discourse is used in three different ways. Democracy as economic freedom (unfettered entrepreneurship) as illustrated by the discourses around women and youth, democracy as political freedom (multiparty politics, free and fair elections) and democracy as governance, civic action and deliberation. In this section I discuss how these last two are used as tropes for the rise of the continent.

The aforementioned 1997 G7 Denver convention highlighted that over 20 African nations held free and fair elections from 1990 and promised to support those countries that would "promote democracy and good governance, improve the integrity of public institutions, enhance the transparency of government spending, in particular of procurement, and develop national anti-bribery regulations" (Communique, 1997). These ideas became the basis of framing what democracy looks like for African countries. For the countries on the continent considered rising, as will be discussed later, one of the factors that makes them emblems of the rising discourse is how successful they are at neoliberalizing. To be considered successful at neoliberalism countries also need to show success at democratizing. Comaroff and Comaroff (2012) state that:

> Capitalism, to be sure does not require democracy; it has done perfectly well under authoritarian regimes in the past, and continues to do so in many parts of the late modern world. But those nation-states that seek to democratize themselves appear, these days, to require at least the figment of a free market. An elective (or is it electoral?) affinity connects the ballot box to business.
>
> (p. 111)

The connection of "ballot box to business" for African countries is through the adoption of multiparty politics. Multiparty politics is viewed as a mark of democracy as it gives the voter the freedom to choose. The voter's freedom to choose means that political parties have to compete. The assumption here is that if political parties have to compete for votes, their manifestos and policies will cater more to the needs of the voter; hence, the quality of government and governance will improve. Countries that have adopted multiparty politics are thus considered to be doing better politically, hence rising. Here, one can see how this idea of political freedom is informed by neoliberalism.

> At the end of the cold war only three African countries (out of 53 at the time) had democracies; since then the number has risen to 25, of varying shades, and many more countries hold imperfect but worthwhile elections (22 in 2012 alone). Only four out of now 55 countries – Eritrea, Swaziland, Libya and Somalia – lack a multi-party constitution, and the last two will get one soon. Armies mostly stay in their barracks. Big-man leaders are becoming rarer, though some authoritarian states survive. And on the whole more democracy has led to better governance: politicians who want to be re-elected need to show results.
>
> ("*The hopeful continent*", 2011)

Another mark of democracy as political freedom is the ability of countries to conduct free and fair elections. Grugel and Bishop (2013) and Lindberg (2006) note that elections in African countries are a means of evaluating progress and development as they show how successful or unsuccessful, countries are at democratizing. Elections are a significant part of the process of neoliberalism as they represent "the ultimate symbol of a successful transition" (Cheeseman, 2015, p. 117) into governments that would be effective, cultivating an environment for economic growth, poverty reduction and conflict resolution. How successful a country is at conducting an election – that is, how free and fair an election is – reflects how politically progressive a country is, hence, rising.

> African governments are beginning to accept the importance of good governance, not least for improving the lot of the poor. Rulers travelling on presidential planes strut their stuff at the World Economic Forum in Davos and declare their undying interest in "capacity-building". Behind the jargon a remarkable change is taking place. The default means of allocating power in Africa now is to hold elections, and elections are generally becoming fairer. Septics rightly bemoan voter fraud and intimidation, and plenty of polls are still stolen. But the margins of victory that autocrats dare to award themselves are shrinking. Indeed, quite a few have discovered, in forced retirement, that by allowing national democracy they have started something they cannot stop.

The excerpt above shows the weight democratic elections are given in showing how far African countries have come in terms of electing leaders. Even though there is still a hint of skepticism, the general tone of the above excerpt glorifies the idea that countries which have successful elections are doing well on the continent. Harrison (2013) argues that the promotion of democracy in African countries was only a means to an end, where the function of democracy through multiparty politics was to put regimes that would promote neoliberal reforms in power. Democratization was "largely 'performative'; that is, the shift toward multipartyism has been orchestrated in a way that allows for substantial continuity in the management of neoliberal reform and minimizes the substance of enfranchisement on African populations" (Harrison, 2013, p. 50). For African countries, displaying characteristics of democracy is one way to show donors their commitment to reform. Democracy is promoted because it creates the right conditions for neoliberal reform to take place as indicated by the excerpt below.

> All this is happening partly because Africa is at last getting a taste of peace and decent government. For three decades after African countries threw off their colonial shackles, not a single one (bar the Indian Ocean island of Mauritius) peacefully ousted a government or president at the ballot box. But since Benin set the mainland trend in 1991, it has happened more than 30 times – far more often than in the Arab world.
>
> ("*The hopeful continent*", 2011)

Democracy as Governance, Civic Action and Deliberation

In addition to having free and fair elections, countries within the continent are considered rising based on the extent to which citizens are able to participate in deliberation and civic action. This is a significant aspect within the rising discourse, especially since dictatorship was one of the issues highlighted within the Afro-pessimistic discourse. To be considered rising, African countries thus need to display devolution of power. This is represented using the presence of functioning local governments, or supporters of different political parties able to coexist with one another reflecting a healthy multiparty environment. The ability of citizens to protest poor governance is also highlighted as an instance of the growth of democracy, with the Arab Spring cited. Democracy is also talked about in relation to having institutions that are trustworthy and that work, enabling leaders to govern effectively.

> It's not the people themselves, but how they work with one another, and with groups and institutions. "The history of Mali is marked by the trust people have in these dealings, institutionalized in the traditional "palaver tree" approach to decision making, where village

> elders consult under a tree until a consensus is reached. Since its creation in 1993, Mali's Decentralization Mission has been educating the public about a modern democratic version of such local control. The country is divided into eight regions, 50 districts, 701 communes and thousands of villages. District chiefs are no longer appointed from the capital of Bamako but elected locally. Later this year, the communes will hold elections. "Reinforcing democracy," says President Konare, "means devolution of power to the communities".
>
> (McGreary & Michaels, 1998)

Although the rise of Africa is attributed to the growth of Western democracy, much skepticism is expressed about the potential of African countries to fully democratize. In some instances, there is a conflation between political stability or instability and the presence or absence of democracy. These tensions and contradictions within the rising discourse will be discussed in the concluding chapter. As demonstrated in this chapter, media institutions and development organizations draw on key ideas, symbols and tropes to justify Africa Rising as a worthy object of inquiry. As Kristof (2012) states, "All in all, though, Africa is becoming more democratic, more technocratic and more market friendly. Yet Americans are largely oblivious to the idea of Africa as a success story".

Other Visual and Discursive Constructions of the Continent

Apart from the images of women and children as symbols/tropes of the rising discourse, other visual constructions used to depict the rise of the continent have included animals and trees. For instance, in their December 3, 2012, "Africa Rising" issue, *Time*, had on the cover page the silhouette of a Baobab tree, against the background of a silhouette of the skyline of a city. The Baobab tree here is symbolic as it is considered as an icon of the African savannah and is referred to as the "tree of life" or "symbol of life" (Aduna, n.d.) due to its capacity to withstand drought. It is found in various African countries and is thus used as a symbol that can speak for the continent. The use of the Baobab tree as a symbol of Africa's rise carries a connotation that despite the continent's perils, it has been able to survive harsh conditions like the Baobab tree and is now thriving. The words "Africa Rising" appear at the top of the tree with "Africa" in bold black font and "Rising" in bold white font. Next to these words reads a description: "it's the world's next economic powerhouse. But huge challenges lie ahead" ("*Africa Rising*", 2012). On March 2, 2013, *The Economist*'s issue of "*Aspiring Africa*" had a silhouette of a giraffe with the size of its neck appearing twice the size of a normal giraffe's neck. The silhouette of the giraffe towers above a background of trees and what looks like the sky at the break of dawn or dusk. McKinsey Global Institute, the business and economics research branch of McKinsey & Company, American global firm, did a report in 2010 titled "Lions on the move: The progress and potential of African Economies", with the images on the cover page a construction worker with a construction vehicle in the background, a young girl using a mobile phone and a man in a laboratory. In 2016 the company produced another report, "*Lions on the move II: Realizing the potential of Africa's Economies*" with the image on the cover page that of a city with skyscrapers. In February 2018, Ipsos, a marketing and research firm, released a report "*African Lions: Who are Africa's Middle Class?*" This report had a plain cover page. All of these news and institutional reports produced at different times rely on visual symbols and words to express the rise of the continent. Parameswaran (2002) states,

> Business and news magazine and nonfiction book cover images, which bridge the aesthetics of journalism, high art, and commercial mass production, seek to accomplish multiple tasks simultaneously: they try to sell the promise and personality of the magazine or book, convey the crux or essence of the discourse story in visual form, and stimulate the curiosity of potential readers in online and offline retail consumer environments.
>
> (p. 518)

Parameswaran (2002) additionally notes that "animals/bestial embodiments" are part of the symbolic currency used within the global financial markets, to visually construct emerging economies, "Reductionist visual binaries of optimistic bulls and pessimistic bears have long signified the seemingly schizophrenic fluctuations of the Western capitalist market economy" (p. 518). The visual and discursive constructions of the rise of Africa rely on animal symbolism such as the lion and the giraffe. These images of animals and trees are used in the service of the rising discourse to rebrand the image of the continent as fierce, strong and powerful and not "the hopeless continent" it was once considered to be. The images of the giraffe with the very elongated neck and the Baobab tree towering above a city are used to signify the potential of the continent to grow. The neck of the giraffe and, as discussed earlier, the child flying a rainbow-colored kite with the shape of the continent invoke Rostow's earlier discussed (1959) stages of economic growth model, by visually constructing the take-off stage – a stage characterized by intense technological growth and political stability, captured by the rising discourse. The visual and discursive constructions of the continent begin to reveal how the rising discourse is enmeshed in a complex web of global power relations.

In conclusion, this chapter shows how the various key terms, images, recurring tropes and metaphors used in depicting Africa as rising rely on historical representations of the continent as pessimistic to make Africa's rise make sense. It also shows how some of these tropes are deeply embedded in the global imaginary as normalized ways of talking about Africa.

References

Aduna. (n.d.). *The Baobab Tree: Africa's Iconic "Tree of Life"*. Retrieved from https://aduna.com/blogs/learn/the-baobab-tree

A hopeful continent. (2013, March 2). *The Economist*, *406*(8825), 3(US). General OneFile.

Africa rising; The hopeful continent. (2011, December 3). *The Economist*, *401*(8762), 15(US). General OneFile.

Akabor, N. (2023, November 2). *The rise of African tech hubs: How they are becoming the silicon valleys of the Continent.* https://www.cnbcafrica.com/2023/the-rise-of-african-tech-hubs-how-they-are-becoming-the-silicon-valleys-of-the-continent/

Appadurai, A. (1990). Disjuncture and difference in the global cultural economy 1990. *Cultural Theory: An Anthology*, *2011*, 282–295.

Aspiring Africa. (n.d.). *The Economist.* Retrieved August 19, 2024, from https://www.economist.com/leaders/2013/03/02/aspiring-africa

Boserup, E. (1975). *The changing role of women in developing countries on JSTOR.* https://www.jstor.org/stable/23001836?casa_token=8rAhev6Di28AAAAA:GTnMWzlrZKQsJ2FmT-VjA-J-h-3sDVv8PctYTdM29ttzBKeqMUESOj5i1rF5fmQDpOuiAeWATePWMMG8qsW4TyUfqL2fhiukKBL9e-h4tLuySajmW7U

Bughin, J. (2016). *Lions on the move II: Realizing the potential of Africa's economies.* McKinsey Global Institute.

Burke, K. (1966). *Language as symbolic action: Essays on life, literature, and method.* University of California Press.

Cheeseman, N. (2015). *Democracy in Africa: Successes, failures, and the struggle for political reform* (Vol. 9). Cambridge University Press.

Comaroff, J., & Comaroff, J. L. (2012). Theory from the South: Or, how Euro-America is evolving toward Africa. *Anthropological Forum*, *22*, 113–131.

Connors, W. (2011, January 18). In Nigeria, used cars are a road to status. *Wall Street Journal.* https://www.wsj.com/articles/SB10001424052748704515904576076622892749928

Denver Summit of the Eight: Communique. (n.d.). Retrieved July 1, 2024, from https://1997–2001.state.gov/issues/economic/summit/communique97.html

Doing it my way; Ethiopia and Kenya. (2013, March 2). *The Economist*, *406*(8825), 12(US). General OneFile.

Emerging Africa. (1997, June 12). *The Economist*, *343*(8021), 13-. General OneFile.

Grugel, J., & Bishop, M. L. (2013). *Democratization: A critical introduction.* Macmillan International Higher Education.

Harrison, G. (2013). *Neoliberal Africa: The impact of global social engineering.* Zed Books Ltd.
Kleinman, A., & Kleinman, J. (1996). The appeal of experience; The dismay of images: Cultural appropriations of suffering in our times. *Daedalus*, *125*(1), 1–23.
Kristof, N. (2007, July 5). *Africa: Land of hope—The New York Times.* https://www.nytimes.com/2007/07/05/opinion/05kristof.html
Kristof, N. (2012, June 30). *Africa on the rise—The New York Times.* https://www.nytimes.com/2012/07/01/opinion/sunday/africa-on-the-rise.html
Lerner, D. (1958). *The passing of traditional society: Modernizing the Middle East.* http://psycnet.apa.org/psycinfo/1959-08081-000
Lindberg, S. I., & Lindberg, S. (2006). *Democracy and elections in Africa.* JHU Press.
Making Africa work; Business in Africa. (2016, April 16). *The Economist*, *419*(8985), 10(US). General OneFile.
Massey, D. (2007). *World city.* Polity.
McDubus, C. (2017, November 22). Smart cities evolving: Where is Rwanda today? *Africa-OnTheRise.* https://www.africa-ontherise.com/2017/11/smart-cities-evolving-where-is-rwanda-today/
Mcgeary, J., & Michaels, M. (1998, March 30). Africa rising. *Time*, *151*(12), 34–44.
Miller, C., & Razavi, S. (1995). *From WID to GAD: Conceptual shifts in the women and development discourse* (No. 1). UNRISD Occasional Paper.
Musau, Z. (n.d.). *Global companies give Africa a second look | Africa Renewal Online.* Retrieved November 17, 2018, from https://www.un.org/africarenewal/magazine/august-november-2017/global-companies-give-africa-second-look
Nothias, T. (2014). 'Rising','hopeful','new': Visualizing Africa in the age of globalization. *Visual Communication*, *13*(3), 323–339.
Parameswaran, R. (2002). Local culture in global media: Excavating colonial and material discourses in National Geographic. *Communication Theory*, *12*(3), 287–315.
Rostow, W. W. (1959). The stages of economic growth. *The Economic History Review*, *12*(1), 1–16.
Roxburgh, C., Dörr, N., Leke, A., Tazi-Riffi, A., Van Wamelen, A., Lund, S., Chironga, M., Alatovik, T., Atkins, C., & Terfous, N. (2010). Lions on the move: The progress and potential of African economies. *McKinsey Global Institute*, 1–8.
The Baobab: Africa's Tree of Life. (2018, June 29). *Asilia Africa.* https://www.asiliaafrica.com/the-baobab-africas-tree-of-life/
The gateway to Africa? South Africa. (2012, June 2). *The Economist*, *403*(8787), 62(US). General OneFile.
The new champions. (2008, September 20). *The Economist*, *388*(8598), 6(US). General OneFile.
The Role of Cities in Africa's Rise. (n.d.). KPMG International.
TIME Magazine Cover: Africa Rising—Dec. 3, 2012—Africa—Economy. (n.d.). Retrieved August 19, 2024, from https://content.time.com/time/covers/europe/0,16641,20121203,00.html

van Blerk, H., & Mwaura, N. (2018). *African lions: Who are Africa's rising middle class?* Ipsos. https://www.ipsos.com/en/african-lions-who-are-africas-rising-middle-class

What technology can do for Africa. (n.d.). Retrieved August 19, 2024, from https://www.economist.com/special-report/2017/11/10/what-technology-can-do-for-africa

Wilkins, K. G. (2016). Communication, Gender, and Development. In Communicating Gender and Advocating Accountability in Global Development (pp. 1–42). Springer.

Wonacott, P. (2011, January 13). A continent of new consumers beckons; as disposable incomes continue to climb, multinationals shift focus from resources to retail. *The Wall Street Journal Eastern Edition*, B1. General OneFile.

3 “Afrocentric” Digital Platforms and the Rising Discourse

Previous scholarship on the rise of the African continent has mainly focused on how Anglo-American media institutions have articulated the discourse of “Africa Rising”. But how does Afrocentric media engage with this discourse? This study defines what Afrocentric media are, how they have emerged, their role in shaping perceptions about the continent and its diaspora, how they engage with both the pessimistic and the rising discourses and what they reveal about globalization in African countries. These questions are addressed using data collected by interviews conducted with 20 contributors of “Afrocentric” digital platforms that included some founders, editors, writers and photographers. It also includes web pages of these platforms as part of the analysis to examine what kinds of stories these platforms focus on. To begin with, why the term “Afrocentric” digital platforms? Here I draw on the theory of “Afrocentricity” by Asante (1991) as cited by Mazama (2001, p. 388) stating,

> As an intellectual theory, Afrocentricity is the study of the ideas and events from the standpoint of Africans as the key players rather than victims. This theory becomes, by virtue of an authentic relationship to the centrality of our own reality, a fundamentally empirical project ... it is Africa asserting itself intellectually and psychologically, breaking the bonds of Western domination in the mind as an analogue for breaking those bonds in every other field.

With the above definition in mind, I define “Afrocentric digital platforms” as online platforms with the aim to challenge the normative representations of the African continent and its diaspora in mainstream global media. These include sites such as *AfricasaCountry*, *ThisisAfrica*, *OkayAfrica*, *EverydayAfrica*, *Africa-ontherise*, *Face2FaceAfrica*, *Kibera Stories*, *Gova-Media*, *Ayiba Magazine* and *Afrobloggers*, among others. They represent one way in which Africa is “asserting itself intellectually and psychologically”. This notion of Afrocentricity within these

DOI: 10.4324/9781003472124-3

platforms is expressed in their goals, vision and mission statements. For instance, the platform *This is Africa* has its slogan as "fresh insights on Africa by Africans" ("About This is Africa", 2019) and its mission as "To reclaim and define our identity, our heritage and our continent's rightful political, economic and cultural position in the globalised world and in the global consciousness" ("About This is Africa", 2019).

Similarly, *Everyday Africa* provides a space where photographers from various countries within the continent upload their pictures to showcase what daily life is like in those places. For this platform it is important to showcase what everyday life in various parts of the continent looks like to demonstrate that the extreme depictions of war poverty and disease are not as prevalent as one would think. While the mission of *Everyday Africa* does not explicitly allude to "Africa Rising", another platform *Africa on the Rise* is explicit in its mission, stating,

> Africa-OnTheRise is committed to highlighting and propagating the positive changing realities of the African continent. This platform is changing the African conversation by monitoring, analyzing, and sharing qualitative content about Africa's rising potential, fostering development through the power of information and inspiring hope by humanizing the process of positive change.
>
> ("About Africa-OnTheRise", 2019)

Information and Communication Technologies in Africa

The affordances of ICTs in developing nations were heralded as leapfrogging development and became a key topic within development discourse, as ICTs were considered central to the implementation of development initiatives (Unwin, 2009). The notion that ICTs could transform developing nations was championed in the belief that ICTs would bridge the digital divide enabling developing countries that lagged behind technologically to catch up (Kleine & Unwin, 2009). Bridging the digital divide was viewed as a way to reduce the economic disparities between developed and developing nations. This has led to national governments adopting policies that put ICTs at the heart of their development agendas and companies that manufacture technologies capitalizing on this, resulting in what was called the digital revolution (Kleine & Unwin, 2009). The digital revolution in African countries has also been tied to the notion of democracy, where ICTs have been characterized as not only giving voice to citizens but also as allowing governments to serve better their citizens through e-governance and thus e-democracy (Banda, Mudhai & Tettey, 2009). The push for ICTs in developing countries was done from a modernization standpoint that suggested that technological modernization would lead to development. The notion that ICTs were the panacea to underdevelopment was criticized as being technologically deterministic and Eurocentric.

The significance of ICTs in African countries cannot, however, be downplayed within the "Africa Rising" discourse, as it is through these ICTs that Africans have been able to connect with each other and other parts of the world playing a role in the globalization process (Ogan et al., 2009). While ICTs encompass different kinds of technologies ranging from computers to agricultural technologies that can increase production, mobile phones in developing countries are seen as a significant technology under Information and Communication Technologies for Development (ICT4D). In addition to social networking and being used for public health purposes, mobile phones have also been viewed as opening up spaces for "e-democracy" by providing citizens with information, opportunities for campaigning, and facilitating the monitoring of elections (Wasserman, 2011, 2016). The innovative ways in which Africans have appropriated the mobile phone into their lives while also creating technology to serve their needs represents a participatory aspect of ICT4D, where people participate in their own development. This is demonstrated through the growth of technology start-ups in countries such as Kenya, which is currently branded the "Silicon Savannah" in reference to Silicon Valley in the United States (Gathigi & Waititu, 2012; Hussey, 2015; Perry, 2011), becoming a significant trope of the "Africa Rising" discourse. It is thus important to examine how the digital revolution on the African continent is depicted within this discourse.

The proliferation of ICTs, together with the liberalization of the airwaves, created a space where Africans have been able to produce, distribute and share their own content. This content articulates what it means to be African or grow up on the continent and depicts the continent as "rising", while also functioning as a site where Africans negotiate their own identities in relation to the rest of the world. This is an important part of the Afropolitan identity that I further discuss later. Mbembe in an interview with Haak (2015) speaks of the revolutionizing aspect of mobile phones on the African continent, stating that mobile phones have provided a means for Africans to relate to themselves, to each other, and to understand themselves better even as they connect with the rest of the world.

ICTs and their role for development have been discussed in terms of economic growth through entrepreneurship, education, e-health, e-governance and rural development (Unwin, 2009). One of the other affordances ICTs have provided is enabling Africans to speak on their own behalf through hashtags such as #theafricatheynevershowyou, #everydayafrica or blogs, vlogs and social media continent that aim at showing the normalcy of life in various parts of the continent and narrate the different ways that Africans participate in their own advancement. The proliferation of digital technologies and the internet in African countries has been viewed as a significant part of the Afropolitan consciousness (Mbembe & Balakrishnan, 2016; Pahl, 2016). As Gehrmann (2016) states, "the success of the Afropolitan generation nor the controversy around the concept would have been possible without the cyberspace as a new venue for mobility in the sense of the circulation, of ideas, images, and self-celebration" (p. 63). The affordances of ICTs for economic growth and the subsequent digital cultures such as Afropolitanism are thus an interesting site to explore how the "Africa Rising" discourse might have been shaped by these factors.

Afropolitanism and Afrocentric Media

When Lerner (1958) put forth the idea of "information transfer" as a means to assist developing nations to catch up with developed nations, he did not anticipate how media technologies would evolve in both developed and developing nations, providing new ways of articulating individual, community and national identities. Articulating these identities has become a significant way of challenging the dominant development discourse that stipulated those developing nations had been left behind. Media technologies in African countries have become an important part of resisting and challenging dominant discourses about countries in the African continent. This resistance has emerged from the idea of Afropolitanism, which Pahl (2016) contends "acknowledges a certain position *in* the world but expresses a certain disposition *towards* the world" (p. 74). Eze (2014) argues that Afropolitanism is a critical concept that reshapes the self-perception, position and subjectivity of the African identity from one that is characterized by victimhood and defined through and by European identity to more nuanced identities that blur cultural lines, forming subjects that are multiethnic, multiracial and transcultural. These identities, Eze (2014) argues, are shaped "by relation rather than in opposition" to other identities. Gehrmann (2016) further explains that Afropolitanism is also characterized by "digital mobility which encompasses a quick circulation of ideas and images via the cyberspace that characterizes both the construction and contestation of Afropolitan lifestyles and cultural production" (p. 61). This notion of digital mobility connects with Lerner's (1958) argument that modernization can be linked to physical mobility that happens as people move from one place to another, experiencing other worlds. Similarly, those who are unable to, media affords them mobility as they experience other worlds without physically traveling.

Roles of Afrocentric Digital Platforms

Afrocentric digital platforms have mushroomed in the past decade both within and outside the continent. As communication technologies and the internet have spread in parts of the continent, more people have gained the ability to begin to tell their own stories, as evidenced through the growth of Afrocentric platforms. So, what is the role of these growing platforms in the construction of Africa's media image in the digital world? There was consensus among the participants I spoke to about the prevalence and persistence of the Afro-pessimistic discourse and the need for alternative representations of the continent. In discussion with the founders and contributors of these platforms, two main themes began to emerge on what they see the role these platforms play in shaping perceptions of the continent. These themes are social responsibility and policing the representation of the continent.

Social Responsibility and Digitally Policing the Narrative

In conversation with founders, editors and contributors of Afrocentric digital platforms on why they began or why they contribute to such platforms, they saw these platforms and their contributions as a duty and social responsibility to African countries, cultures, identities that has been mostly associated with the dominant Afro-pessimistic discourse. These contributors saw it as their duty to rewrite and reclaim the narratives about the African continent and push against the Afro-pessimistic discourse. For instance, one participant who lived in Ivory Coast as part of the Peace Corps and later worked as a photographer in Ivory Coast explains the tensions they experienced documenting Ivory Coast's recovery from the civil war stating,

> While we were there, we began to get very frustrated because we sort of realized that this was more the same, it was an important story, it was a true story but it was yet another piece on refugees, chaos, conflict, crisis and we felt that despite the fact that it was an important piece that was underreported it was not as important what we knew to be true about that part of the continent from the long time that we lived there, which is that for the vast majority of people, the vast majority of time life's very normal. So, it's not to discount the importance of the crisis piece that we are there for, but we felt that the more important thing was to try and find a way to show people what you never see, which is images and stories regarding everyday life. And the challenge was to try and find a way to make the everyday interesting, to make the normal sort of everyday activities of life beautiful, interesting fun to look at engaging.

These founders and contributors to these platforms see themselves as doing their part in telling stories about various aspects of African countries and influencing perceptions. They see it as their responsibility to do so as they have an insider's perspective on what life in various parts of the continent and its diaspora is like.

They also see telling stories that focus on various other aspects of African countries not simplified versions of Afro-pessimism as the only reality on the continent – as their responsibility. Even with stories that focus on tragedies on the continent, they see their role as providing more nuanced and complex representations of these issues and not the simplified and generalized versions found in some mainstream media platforms. The crowdsourced nature of these platforms, that is, having contributors from various parts of the continent and diaspora, coupled with this sense of social responsibility allows for more nuanced coverage that shows the complex nature of issues affecting the continent. The notion of social responsibility becomes even more amplified since most of the contributors to these platforms do not get financially compensated for it. The political economic aspect of these platforms in some cases becomes a challenge because it becomes difficult to find contributors who will not expect to be paid. Additionally, contributors in some instances do not feel the pressure to meet deadlines because in any case they do not get compensated financially. Given the political and economic constraints of these platforms, those who choose to contribute without expecting to be paid for it see it as a social responsibility and see their work as playing a crucial role in shaping perceptions about the continent. While contributors argue that it would be nice to earn from it, they see more value in being able to offer alternative perspectives about African countries, cultures and identities.

Apart from seeing their contributions to Afrocentric digital platforms as a social responsibility, they also see these platforms as digitally policing the representations of the African continent, cultures and experience. Here, these platforms play a watchdog role on how mainstream media covers affairs of various African countries. Some contributors noted that because these platforms currently exist, mainstream media or other platforms are slowly becoming conscious of how they represent African countries. This is mainly because of how Afrocentric digital platforms take a critical stance toward how mainstream media and other platforms discuss issues about African countries. One interviewee stated:

> I think we pushback and we challenge, and we make them self-reflect because I think we have a lot of journalists who follow us and they are kind of wary of what...is going to say about this, that or the other thing.

This is also because audiences turn to Afrocentric platforms to see what the latter think about a specific piece that was done by mainstream media that may be considered Afro-pessimistic, or what they think about specific issues. There is an unspoken expectation that these Afrocentric platforms will challenge media that promotes Afro-pessimism and hence offer alternative viewpoints or more nuanced coverage. Thus, media outlets that cover and produce content about African countries and affairs begin to become cognizant of how they portray the continent.

Although this is not the case for all media covering the continent, Afrocentric platforms can be seen as subtly playing a watchdog role in how the continent is represented. As more of these platforms begin to emerge and become popular, apart from policing the narrative, one of the founders of one of these platforms highlights that they also get consulted by mainstream media platforms for their expertise on African affairs. In some cases, these platforms also play an agenda-setting role as mainstream media are influenced in what they write about regarding the continent. Apart from responding and critiquing coverage by other media platforms, some editors noted that they get consulted as experts on African issues. They stated that whenever news breaks about various issues in African countries, not only do audiences interested in alternative perspectives turn to these platforms, but also mainstream media in some instances reach out to the editors of these platforms for their expertise. The growing following on various social media sites with platforms such as *Africasacountry* amassing more than 90,000 followers on Twitter, and *Everyday Africa* with over 300,000 followers on Instagram, is an indicator of a desire for alternative perspectives. Due to their contributions to these Afrocentric platforms, the contributors' work becomes more visible, leading to some of them getting contacted to contribute pieces in mainstream media.

By becoming part of the conversation about African affairs and bringing in alternative viewpoints to mainstream media these digital platforms are indirectly influencing conversations about African affairs in mainstream media. Although these crossovers or dialogues between these digital platforms and mainstream media are not very common, they need to be recognized when they happen as moments of rupture that allow for alternative viewpoints about African countries to circulate in mainstream media and as moments during which Afrocentric digital platforms are playing a part in shaping perceptions about the continent. Here, Afrocentric digital platforms can also be seen as fulfilling the agendas of the NWICO debates discussed in Chapter 1, where countries in the non-aligned movement wanted among other things, fair representation from media in the Global North. Afrocentric digital platforms can be seen as especially fulfilling the goals of news agencies such as Pan African News Agency (PANA) established by the Organization of

African Union (OAU) after the failure of the NWICO debates to challenge the Afro-pessimistic representation. Although, PANA did not last as it ran into challenges of language barriers across the continent and legitimacy in the eyes of news agencies in Western countries. While Afrocentric digital platforms are not without similar challenges, as highlighted by the founders and contributors interviewed, their emergence in the past 10 to 15 years reiterates the goals of the NWICO debates and PANA as they seek to challenge pessimistic representations of the continent. For example, a platform like *Face2FaceAfrica* states in its mission

> Face2face Africa is a premier pan-African digital media and events company based in New York City. Our mission is to reshape the pan-African narrative and amplify the voice of black people around the globe. Our digital platforms and events reach, engage, and connect millions of audiences each year.
>
> ("About Face2FaceAfrica", 2019)

These platforms can therefore be considered a renaissance of the NWICO debates and PANA. But how do Afrocentric digital platforms view their work in relation to the "Africa Rising" discourse, especially if their aim is to challenge the Afro-pessimistic discourse?

Situating Afrocentric Digital Platforms Within Discourses About Africa

While there is consensus on the role that Afrocentric digital platforms play or can play in regard to influencing perceptions about African affairs, these platforms do not exist in a vacuum and, therefore, influence and are influenced by discourses about the African continent. These platforms emerged as a response to the dominant Afro-pessimistic discourse that created the desire for alternative viewpoints about the continent and its affairs. They emerge as a form of resistance to the pessimistic discourse, as they seek to dismantle it and present alternative perspectives about the continent and its affairs. These platforms, therefore, embody a postcolonial agenda with their emancipatory stance and desire to reclaim and rewrite the narratives about African countries. For instance, the names of some of these platforms are one way of symbolically challenging the Afro-pessimistic discourse. For example, *Africasacountry* evokes irony as it critiques the perception of the continent as a homogenous entity. *OkayAfrica* suggests that the continent is not the place of doom that has been considered to be. *ThisisAfrica,* in its aim to challenge the Afro-pessimistic discourse, tells its readers that this is what the continent is really about. From their names, goals and missions stated earlier, one can see that the emergence of these platforms is influenced by the Afro-pessimistic discourse. But are these platforms influenced by the rising discourse? Here, I posit that the conditions that led to the emergence of the rising discourse about Africa – that is neoliberal restructuring, also contributed to the emergence of Afrocentric digital platforms. Although neoliberal reform is not the only condition contributing to the emergence of these platforms, one can argue that it was a catalyst as it influenced changes that allowed for the proliferation of privately run media institutions. Through the push for privatization and democracy, it became important to create an environment that allowed for the growth of media institutions. As discussed in Chapter 2, one of the signs of a healthy democracy in African countries is/was the condition of media institutions in those countries. As discussed in Chapter 4, democracy is one of the tropes of rising countries. Therefore, countries that wanted to look democratic had to support a media model that allows for a multiplicity of voices. It is within this environment of libertarianism that Afrocentric digital platforms emerged. While some of the Afrocentric platforms are based in the diaspora, because these platforms also rely on contributors based on the continent, most of these contributors end up being from countries that have more libertarian media model. As such, in interviewing the founders and contributors and looking at articles on these platforms, I found that most of the contributors are from countries such as Ghana, Nigeria, South Africa, Kenya, Ethiopia, Senegal and countries that have more liberalized media. This is not to say that the relationship between the government and media institutions in these countries is without challenges, but governments have allowed for the growth of other media institutions. Indeed, this notion also came up in conversation with founders and editors of these platforms, who noted that most of their contributors tend to come from African countries that have more media freedom.

Apart from media freedom, contributors to these platforms based in African countries are also crowdsourced from countries with better digital connectivity. Nyabola (2018) states, "those who are making politics online are a subset of a subset of yet another subset – those who have access to electricity, those who have access to the internet, and finally those who have accounts on social media" (p. 101). Based on this, one can also argue that indeed the growth of the middle class in African countries has also influenced the growth of these Afrocentric platforms. It is, therefore, not surprising that Afrocentric digital platforms have more of an audience reach and contributors from countries considered as rising, as these countries have conditions that facilitate the access of these platforms. While this is not an intentional goal of the founders and editors of these platforms, as they desire to have contributors and audiences in all parts of the continent, it is interesting to see how this pattern of where the majority of their audiences and contributors are based on the continent, mirror the countries considered as the rising ones such as South Africa, Kenya, Ghana, etc. Additionally, some of the content carried by these platforms reflects the tropes of the rising discourse such as entrepreneurship, democracy and women's empowerment, as one of the founders/editors stated:

> I focus a lot on entrepreneurship, 60% of the content that we have is entrepreneurship based. We also have the economic side of the website that takes a lot of space in the sense that every governmental decision that positively impact the continent we will share about it, so it could be any decision made by a country to facilitate trade between neighboring countries for as it is positive for the African continent... for us a big part of what we do is speaking to young people because they represent the major driving force of whatever the continent becomes in the next 10–20 years ... what they do essentially is to approach it from an outward in approach, what we do is from the inward out. We shine a light on what is happening locally, and it can be anything from a little us a group of young high school girls who built a generator that is powered by wind and telling you how that speaks to a future or even a present scenario of Africa's technology space.

One can, therefore, argue that the rising discourse implicitly influences the emergence of Afrocentric platforms. How do the founders, editors and contributors of these platforms situate their work in relation to the rising discourse?

Global Flows, Afrocentric Digital Platforms and the Rise of Africa

The emergence of Afrocentric digital platforms represents global dynamics at work, as they are symbolic of global flows – an instance of the local connecting with the global in three ways. First, these platforms themselves are a consequence of global flows. The founders, contributors and audiences are situated in various localities yet connect with each other to share alternative perspectives about African affairs. For instance, some of these platforms are based in the United States or Canada but have contributors and audiences located in African countries and its diaspora, as highlighted earlier. These platforms are, therefore, symbolic of the movement of people. As noted earlier, the people associated with these platforms have various connections to the continent. Second, Afrocentric digital platforms are also a consequence of the flow of technology that has enabled citizens in various African countries to be able to participate on these platforms. Third, as these platforms seek to challenge pessimistic narratives by offering alternative perspectives and by focusing their attention on other things happening on the continent and its diaspora, they facilitate global flows between African countries and outside the continent. By doing this, they highlight various aspects of popular culture such as music, films, sports, etc. while also providing more nuance to other events happening in various countries. Fourth, although these platforms tend to focus more on some countries, they are an instance of translocalization within the continent, as they show how various localities within the continent connect with each other or are different whether through music, food and fashion. The role of these Afrocentric digital platforms, therefore, needs to be taken into consideration in the construction of the continent and its diaspora. These platforms also begin to reveal how Africans and Afropolitans situate their work within the two discourses, showing that the rising discourse is complex and generates various meanings in various contexts.

References

About This is Africa. (2019). *This is Africa.* https://thisisafrica.me/about/

About Us Africa-OnTheRise. (2015, November 16). *Africa-OnTheRise.* https://www.africa-ontherise.com/about-us/

About Us—Face2Face Africa. (n.d.). Retrieved August 27, 2024, from https://face2faceafrica.com/about-us

Asante, M. K. (1991). The Afrocentric idea in education. *The Journal of Negro Education*, *60*(2), 170–180. https://doi.org/10.2307/2295608

Eze, C. (2014). Rethinking African culture and identity: The Afropolitan model. *Journal of African Cultural Studies*, *26*(2), 234–247.

Gathigi, G., & Waititu, E. (2012). Coding for development in the silicon Savannah: The emerging role of digital technology in Kenya. *Re-Imagining Development Communication in Africa*, 201–223.

Gehrmann, S. (2016). Cosmopolitanism with African roots. Afropolitanism's ambivalent mobilities. *Journal of African Cultural Studies*, *28*(1), 61–72.

Haak, B. van der. (2015, August 7). *The internet is Afropolitan.* https://thisisafrica.me/politics-and-society/the-internet-is-afropolitan/

Hussey, M. (2015). Silicon Savannah: How start-ups in Africa are taking on some of humanity's biggest challenges. *Huffington Post.*

Kleine, D., & Unwin, T. (2009). Technological revolution, evolution and new dependencies: What's new about ICT4D? *Third World Quarterly*, *30*(5), 1045–1067.

Lerner, D. (1958). *The passing of traditional society: Modernizing the Middle East.* http://psycnet.apa.org/psycinfo/1959-08081-000

Mazama, A. (2001). The Afrocentric paradigm: Contours and definitions. *Journal of Black Studies*, *31*(4), 387–405. https://doi.org/10.1177/002193470103100401

Mbembe, A., & Balakrishnan, S. (2016). Pan-African legacies, Afropolitan futures. *Transition*, *120*, 28–37. https://doi.org/10.2979/transition.120.1.04

Mudhai, O. F., Tettey, W., & Banda, F. (Eds.). (2009). *African media and the digital public sphere* (1st ed). Palgrave Macmillan.

Nyabola, N. (2018). *Digital democracy, analogue politics: How the internet era is transforming politics in Kenya*. Zed Books. http://ebookcentral.proquest.com/lib/templeuniv-ebooks/detail.action?docID=5567836

Ogan, C. L., Bashir, M., Camaj, L., Luo, Y., Gaddie, B., Pennington, R., Rana, S., & Salih, M. (2009). Development communication the state of research in an era of ICTs and globalization. *International Communication Gazette*, *71*(8), 655–670.

Pahl, M. (2016). Afropolitanism as critical consciousness: Chimamanda Ngozi Adichie's and Teju Cole's internet presence. *Journal of African Cultural Studies*, *28*(1), 73–87.

Perry, A. (2011, June 30). Silicon Savanna: Mobile phones transform Africa. *Time*. http://content.time.com/time/magazine/article/0,9171,2080702,00.html

Unwin, P. T. H. (2009). *ICT4D: Information and communication technology for development*. Cambridge University Press.

Wasserman, H. (2011). Mobile phones, popular media, and everyday African democracy: Transmissions and transgressions. *Popular Communication*, *9*(2), 146–158.

Wasserman, H. (2016). Shifting power relations, shifting images. *Africa's Media Image in the 21st Century: From the "Heart of Darkness" to "Africa Rising"*, 193.

4 "Active, Dynamic Forces"

Neoliberal Agents and Subjects Within the Africa Rising Discourse

Discourses are articulated and promoted through social actors. Within the representation of the African continent as rising, various social actors play a significant role in the promotion and justification of this discourse. This chapter identifies who these social actors are and what role they play within this discourse. Who is given agency, that is, how various social actors are involved in the discourse of Africa Rising? The social actors represented as active and dynamic forces within the Africa Rising discourse include the African continent, governments, international development and business organizations, other countries in the Global South (China and India) and media institutions. Apart from these, I refer to other actors as secondary social actors, as they are briefly mentioned within the reports but do play a role within this discourse. These include women, youth, elites, returnees and industries. What makes the rising discourse captivating is how these various social actors are situated within it while also advancing it. Below is a table showing the key discourses, metaphors and social actors.

Discourse	*Key Terms and Metaphors*	*Social Actors, Motives*
Afro-pessimism	Darkness, war, poverty, disease, hopelessness, conflict, culture	Colonizers, Imperialists, Governments, Media: Justify extraction of resources
Africa Rising	Growth, entrepreneurship, privatization, democracy, trade, foreign direct investments, partnership, urbanization, middle class, cities, markets, physical and institutional infrastructure, culture	Governments, International Financial Organizations, International Development Organizations, Business Institutions, NGO's, Media, Afrocentric Digital Platforms, BRICS. Promote neoliberal globalization

DOI: 10.4324/9781003472124-4

Van Leeuwen (2013) states that, "representations can endow social actors with either active or passive roles. Activation occurs when social actors are represented as the active, dynamic forces in an activity, passivation when they are represented as 'undergoing' the activity, or as being 'at the receiving end of it'" (p. 43). I argue that the Africa Rising discourse consists of various social actors as listed above, and each of these social actors is either subjected and/or advances the discourse. Each of the social actors has their own unique interests within the discourse, which shows how Africa is enmeshed in economic and geopolitical power structures.

Africa as a Social Actor

While there are various social actors listed above that influence the construction of the African continent as rising, the African continent itself is actively rendered as an agent within this process and construction. While the representation of the continent as a homogenous place is problematic (as will be later discussed), it is valuable to think about how the continent itself is a social actor within the rising discourse and how it is imbued with agency. In Chapter 5, I focus on specific African countries that have been identified as rising, discussing what has led to their distinction as the rising ones and the implications for countries not considered as rising. In Chapter 3, I discuss how Afrocentric media institutions are engaged in the construction of the continent as rising. A focus on these two aspects further elaborates how the African continent itself is an active social actor within this discourse. More broadly speaking, however, the depiction of the African continent as rising, signifying that major transformation and restructuring are taking place within the continent, makes the continent and its people social actors. The continent is represented more as a passive social actor, that is, as "'undergoing' the activity, or as being 'at the receiving end of it'" (Van Leuween, 2013, p. 43), with the activity here being neoliberal reform. For something to rise, there must be a catalyst causing it to do so. For the continent, it is the winds of neoliberalism blowing across the continent, causing it to rise, as suggested by the various reports. To represent Africa as rising therefore means displaying the various ways neoliberalism is unfolding on the continent and "transforming" the continent after a period of Afro-pessimism. This is illustrated through the ways that media, development and business institutions adopt the language of neoliberalism as they present the opportunities on the continent for entrepreneurship, competition and the ways that various individuals and countries are succeeding. This is demonstrated for instance in *Time m*agazine "Africa Rising" edition in 1998, which begins by stating that "a new spirit of self-reliance is taking root among many Africans as they seize control of their destiny, what are they doing right?" Another report states, "poor people once mobilized and provided with value, can create tremendous wealth for business" ("The New Champions", 2008). Another report talks about how "the individual and entrepreneurial drive is present and pushing Africa ahead" (Kulish, 2017). Yet another story states, "more and more African countries are now following the Botswana model of welcoming investors and obeying markets" (Kristof, 2007). All of these instances and various others from reports about the rise of Africa allude to the consequences of neoliberal reform that African countries have adopted, transforming their economies and hence leading to the rise of the continent. Through this complex web of power, the continent is represented as doing the right thing to advance itself and hence acting in its best interest.

Although the terms and conditions for neoliberal reforms are problematic as earlier discussed, the continent is represented as playing an active role and having agency in its advancement. While thinking about the continent as a social actor may be considered problematic owing to the complexity of neoliberal economics, with African countries playing more of a passive role in terms of negotiating the terms and conditions, the role of the continent as a social actor, although passive, needs to be acknowledged. This is because for it to work, neoliberalism as a model for economic growth and development requires a location with the right set of conditions. The African continent and all its challenges articulated through the Afro-pessimistic discourse provided a location with ideal conditions for the forces of neoliberalism to exert themselves. In other words, neoliberalism requires disorder to show off its "transformative" potential through the markets. It operates through the ideology that the markets, by creating notions of democracy and freedom, would fix the failure of state-led development through modernization and dependency. Africa Rising is therefore a way to show the world the transformative effects of neoliberalism on this place that was once condemned as the dark continent. In this regard, by being acted upon by the complex forces of neoliberalism, the continent is involved in its process of rising and hence can be argued as a social actor. Within the continent itself other social actors emerged to advance this neoliberal agenda for the continent.

Governments as Social Actors

Governments of various African countries function as social actors within the rising discourse through their role in accepting neoliberal reform and creating the right conditions for neoliberalism to take place. As noted earlier, neoliberalism requires "disorder" to show its transformative potential which is anchored in the state yielding to the market and opening the potential for new actors; hence it was prescribed as the magic potion to development issues in African countries that would transform their economic landscape. However, for this to happen, neoliberalism also requires both physical and institutional infrastructure through which it can advance its goals and flourish. This relates to the takeoff stage of Rostow's stages of economic growth model (Peet & Hartwick, 2015) which involves setting up the physical and institutional infrastructures for the takeoff stage. Through the creation of these various types of infrastructures, governments and leaders in African countries have played a significant role in the rising discourse with the growth of physical and institutional infrastructure credited for the rise of the continent. These governments and leaders therefore become social actors within the rising discourse by putting in place structures that can support neoliberal reform. In doing so, these governments and their leaders function as technologies of neoliberalism as they are used to promote neoliberalism while creating more structures for it to keep growing. This illustrates Foucault's notion of "governmentality" "the subject who is governed is also at the same time the subject who governs" (Lemm & Vatter, 2017, p. 44). Through adopting neoliberalism, governments in African countries allowed themselves to be governed by global power structures while also governing through neoliberalism by creating structures for it to work. The following quote from one of the rising reports reflects this idea.

> Political freedom, however patchy, is commoner than it was a generation ago. Two-thirds of African countries now limit presidential terms; at least 14 leaders (with a few bad exceptions) have felt obliged to step down as a result. Multi-party systems, however fraught, are more usual; the notion of political accountability and choice is more widely accepted. The media, partly because of the internet, are livelier. The latest index of African governance funded by Mo Ibrahim, a Sudanese-born telecoms mogul, suggests a general improvement.
>
> ("There Is Hope; Africa", 2008)

Another report illustrating how through governmentality, governments in African countries and their leaders are social actors within the rising discourse, states:

> African governments are beginning to accept the importance of good governance, not least for improving the lot of the poor. Rulers travelling on presidential planes strut their stuff at the World Economic Forum in Davos and declare their undying interest in "capacity-building". Behind the jargon a remarkable change is taking place.

> The default means of allocating power in Africa now is to hold elections, and elections are generally becoming fairer. Sceptics rightly bemoan voter fraud and intimidation, and plenty of polls are still stolen. But the margins of victory that autocrats dare to award themselves are shrinking. Indeed, quite a few have discovered, in forced retirement, that by allowing notional democracy they have started something they cannot stop.
>
> (McGreary & Michaels, 1998)

Apart from the importance of institutional infrastructure for a rising continent, the growth of physical infrastructure is also a significant factor as demonstrated by the excerpt below. Physical infrastructure in the form of road networks and rails signifies connectivity and mobility within the continent. This also speaks to South–South relations within the continent as people, goods and media move across country borders.

> Transport management in particular has become much better. A bus ride from Accra across three African borders in one day is instructive. Departing at sunrise, the 15-seater easily crosses into Togo where it passes well-run port installations and warehouses. An hour later it arrives in Benin. The driver ignores the outstretched hands of traffic policemen. After a few more hours the bus reaches Nigeria amid throngs of packed lorries on their way to Onitsha, Africa's largest market. Most of the bus passengers are professionals, including several telecoms engineers who commute weekly. All four countries have sensible transit policies and trade actively with each other.
>
> (Bye-Bye Big Men – Côte d'Ivoire, Ghana and Nigeria, 2013)

Africa's accelerated growth over the past 14 years owes a great deal to improved macroeconomic and political stability and to structural economic reforms. Government action to end armed conflicts, lower inflation and reduce public-sector debt has created a more stable environment for businesses. A range of microeconomic reforms has energized markets. Governments have privatized state-owned enterprises, increased the openness of trade, lowered corporate taxes, strengthened regulatory and legal systems and provided critical physical and social infrastructure (Leke, Lund, Manyika, & Ramaswamy, 2014, p.2).

From the instances above, one can note how the growth of physical and institutional infrastructure works together in measuring the level of growth on the African continent. The relationship between physical infrastructure, institutional infrastructure and economic development has been highlighted by reports from institutions such as the World Bank

(Foster & Briceño-Garmendia, 2009; (Francois, 2007), and this idea that these three are linked is reiterated through the rising discourse. As mentioned earlier, even though the various paradigms of development were conceptualized at different times under different conditions, they have some shared elements. This link between physical and institutional infrastructure therefore echoes Rostow's stages of economic growth model (Peet & Hartwick, 2015), reflecting the "preconditions for take-off" stage that involves building the right frameworks that allow for the takeoff stage. Governments and leaders that have been able to build or strengthen these institutions, that is, establishing the preconditions for takeoff, are viewed as having agency and contributing to the rise of the continent. What this also illustrates is how discourses need physical and institutional infrastructure to work. In this case, Africa Rising discourse which is a result of the neoliberalism discourse needs physical infrastructure in the form of roads, cities, markets and institutional infrastructure such as multiparty elections, anticorruption laws, etc. Because governments are tasked with creating these infrastructures for these discourses to function, they thus are social actors. This also demonstrates how the role of the state is transformed through neoliberalism from having control over economic and political matters as illustrated within the rising discourse, to what Harvey (2007) states as:

> The role of the state is to create and preserve an institutional framework appropriate to such practices. The state has to be concerned, for example, with the quality and integrity of money. It must also set up military, defense, police, and juridical functions required to secure private property rights and to support freely functioning markets. Furthermore, if markets do not exist (in areas such as education, health care, social security, or environmental pollution), then they must be created, by state action if necessary. But beyond these tasks the state should not venture.
>
> (p. 22)

International Development, Financial and Business Organizations

International development, financial and business organizations are social actors within the rising discourse as media institutions rely on them as the experts to make the proclamation that Africa is rising. Reports from these institutions become evidence that media institutions rely on to justify this claim. Apart from media institutions relying on these reports, international development, financial and business organizations wield power in shaping international relations between various regions of the world. As such, these reports that they produce become significant in influencing the way various countries relate with African countries. American-based International Financial Organizations (IFOs) such as the World Bank and International Monetary Fund (IMF) auditing firms such as McKinsey Global Institute, Ernst & Young and KPMG are actively involved in the representation of the African continent as rising. These institutions are used to legitimize the rising discourse through their predictions about the continent as the new kid on the block bursting with opportunities to invest.

> On IMF forecasts Africa will grab seven of the top ten places over the next five years (our ranking excludes countries with a population of less than 10m as well as Iraq and Afghanistan, which could both rebound strongly in the years ahead). Standard Chartered thinks that Africa could become a significant manufacturing centre.
>
> (The Lion Kings? – A More Hopeful Continent, 2011)

> The African Development Bank gave the so-called Africa Rising debate a significant jolt in 2011 with a report declaring that the African middle class had grown to 350 million people in 2010 from 126 million in 1980. The Organization for Economic Cooperation and Development put the figure in 2010 at a mere 32 million, "or roughly the same as Canada".
>
> (Kulish, 2017)

These institutions are social actors because media institutions rely on the reports, and they produce to provide evidence on the rise of the continent. These reports (Bhorat, Kharas, & Pita, 2017; "Deloitte on Africa", 2012; Kulish, 2017; van Blerk & Mwaura, 2018) illustrate the power that these international institutions have in influencing global flows. They focus on various areas that make the continent worth investing in such as the "demographic dividend" (Drummond, Thakoor & Yu, 2014) where they state:

> Africa will account for 80 percent of the projected 4 billion increase in the global population by 2100. The accompanying increase in its working age population creates a window of opportunity, which if properly harnessed, can translate into higher growth and yield a demographic dividend.
>
> (p. 2)

Other reports highlight the need for other countries and institutions to seize the opportunities that the continent presents, "Africa is the world's second-fastest-growing economic region, yet US engagement with the continent is lagging. There is an opportunity to change that" (Leke et al., 2014, p. 1). Yet another report examining the "Shifting Market Frontiers" megatrend states,

> As some areas of the globe become over-farmed, over-populated, or otherwise reach their maximum potential, others gain prominence for their unexploited potential. To ensure future growth, businesses will have to adapt to the changing demographic, economic and technological reality bringing new markets from frontier into the spotlight. "Shifting Market Frontiers: Africa Rising", builds on this framework and analyses the increasing significance of the African market, the diversity of African consumers as well as opportunities and challenges across key consumer industries in Africa.
>
> (Boumphrey & Brehmer, 2017 p. 14)

Some other reports focus on specific industries such as the opportunities in the energy sector (Castellano et al., 2015), technology and internet access ("EY's attractiveness program Africa", 2017; Manyika et al., 2013), partnerships with other countries in the Global South such as China (Sun, Jayaram, & Kassiri, 2017) and India ("Joining hands to unlock Africa's potential", 2014).

By producing and disseminating reports suggesting that African countries are the new business frontier, companies and countries in other parts of the world begin to set their eyes on these rising countries as they plan for their futures. As these companies and countries begin to make investments in the rising African countries, the flow of "scapes" (Appadurai, 1990) begins to happen as finances, ideologies, people, media and technology move from various parts of the globe to African countries to take advantage of the opportunities being advertised. This almost resembles the scramble and partition of the African continent as various European nations sought to occupy regions of the African continent. International financial institutions and development organizations are thus active social actors in the rising discourse as they dictate the global flow of resources as they push investors from one region of the world to another. The role that these reports play in shaping discourses about globalization and global flows cannot be taken for granted.

South–South Relations and Social Actors Within the Global South

While the rise of the continent is mostly associated with countries and organizations based in Europe or in the United States, countries in the Global South are also part of the rising discourse. As mentioned earlier some reports from international financial and business organizations allude to the role of other countries in the rise of Africa. As such, these countries, mainly China and India, can be argued to be social actors within this discourse. Wasserman (2016) states that "the rise of the BRICS alignment of emerging states has had a significant impact on Africa's position in geo-political networks of power and, concomitantly, on the representations of the continent in global media discourses" (p. 197). Indeed, the influence of China in Africa has been discussed extensively as noted in Chapter 2, and their role as social actors in the rising discourse needs to be examined. McKinsey Global Institute produced the report *Dance of the lions and the dragons,* which notes the various ways that China is partnering with African countries and how these partnerships are facilitating growth in economies. Other reports reiterating the influence of China in Africa include (Kristof, 2012; Kristof, 1997; Kulish, 2017; Onishi, 2016). This relationship between these countries in the Global South is in some cases explicitly mentioned as the reason behind the rise of African countries. As earlier noted, the development of physical infrastructure is one of the conditions given for the rise of the continent. Partnerships with China become significant in this regard as they have contributed to the growth of physical infrastructure in various African countries in the form of road networks, rail, etc. For instance the Standard Gauge Railway in Kenya and Ethiopia has been used as one of the markers of the rise of Africa (Agreements Signed for EAC, 2024; Gorecki, 2020; Soy, 2023).

Apart from building infrastructure, these South–South relations also harness the demographic dividend and growing middle class in African countries as goods such as cars are imported from China and India to African countries (Connors, 2011; "The New Champions", 2008) and services such as the telecommunications industry with companies like India's Bharti Airtel in competition for consumers in Kenya (Childress, 2011). Another way these South–South relations are alluded to is in the borrowing of models of economic development, for instance "Doing it my way; Ethiopia and Kenya" (2013) notes how Ethiopia was successfully using a state-led development model like China did with Rwanda borrowing a leaf from Ethiopia.

The interesting thing about these South–South relations is how the rise of these countries is interconnected. For instance, China's influence in African countries is one of the ways it has gained its reputation as a global powerhouse. This resonates with another interesting thing is as much as these South–South relations (countries, companies, etc.) are social actors and have gained credit within the rising discourse, they are also acted upon by the discourse as they seek opportunities to expand their global influence. They are attracted to the African continent because of the opportunities it provides for their own growth. Their interest in the continent can therefore be argued to be a response to the rising discourse causing these entities to move toward the continent where previously the pessimistic discourse dissuaded them.

Media Institutions as Social Actors

Media institutions also play a concrete role as active social actors within the rising discourse in its production, dissemination and consumption. While the production of Africa as rising may be problematic as will be later discussed, this representation of the African continent shows the role that media plays in influencing global power dynamics. It demonstrates how media in shifting the conversations about the continent from pessimistic to optimistic, inviting investors to the continent, plays a significant role in the flow of "scapes" (Appadurai, 1990). What this also demonstrates is how discourses influence how people and institutions "think and act" (Rose, 2016), as the rising discourse draws countries and institutions toward the continent. Pieterse (2009) states, "By echoing free market rhetoric unhindered, the media have contributed to massive, unprecedented transfers of wealth within countries and on a global scale" (p. 4).

Through the rising discourse which echoes the free market discourse, media institutions not only influence the flow of wealth between the African continent and other regions of the world, they influence the flow of ideoscapes as ideologies such as the free market discourse spread across the continent. Technoscapes are firms such as Transsion, a Chinese smartphone firm producing brands like Tecno that are dominating the African market (Marsh, 2018) or Telecom giants setting up shops in various African countries (Childress, 2011). Ethnoscapes are Africans who have lived in the diaspora in various parts of the world returning and people from other parts of the world moving to African countries to set up shop. Mediascapes as content producers from the African continent and its diaspora create and disseminate content alongside other global media entities.

The rising discourse also influences the flow of mediascapes as media institutions themselves gravitate toward this discourse. This is illustrated in how various media institutions have come up with their own rising news reports ("Africa rising; The hopeful continent", 2011; "Emerging Africa", 1997; Mcgeary & Michaels, 1998; "The New Champions", 2008; *The Lion Kings? – A More Hopeful Continent*, 2011) among others. This is another instance of how those involved in the production of this discourse are also influenced by it, with the discourse gaining more prominence as more media institutions produce news reports on the changes happening on the continent. In short, the more media institutions talk about this "progress" in African countries, it has created a buzz in the African branch of media institutions, leading to more of them talking about it. What started as a media buzzword has coalesced into a pattern of knowledge about the continent. The flow of these scapes demonstrates how discourses influence the ways in which people and institutions think and act and reproduce the terms of their own discursive regimes.

Secondary Actors: Women, Youth, Elites and Returnees

While it seems that institutions are given the most agency in terms of the rise of the continent, there have been some instances where specific groups of people or things have been given some agency. As discussed earlier in Chapter 4, various tropes have been used to discuss the rise of the continent. Among these have included women, youth, children, the middle class and cities, who can also be considered as social actors within this discourse. By virtue of them being displayed as tropes for a rising continent, they also function as social actors. The growing middle class and the youth demographic dividend which are flaunted as reasons why African countries are among the fastest growing and why other global players should pay attention to the continent make them an active and dynamic force within this discourse. More importantly, their role as social actors is enmeshed in how they function both as neoliberal agents and subjects as they advance neoliberalism through their actions, while also being acted upon by the discourse. This is reflected in the way they are talked about within the rising discourse as becoming more self-reliant by starting their own businesses or their increasing purchase power as they gravitate and spend their money on global brands that have made their way to the African markets, or the consumerism that comes with capitalism, "But in a nation where per capita income is about $2,700 a year, most Nigerians still opt for used cars, making the same sort of transition from subsistence earning to consumer spending that plays out across Africa's developing economies" (Connors, 2011).

Another group that is given some agency within the rising discourse is professionals who constitute the growing middle class. Additionally, people living in the diaspora returning back to the continent are also secondary social actors within this discourse as they are used to show how the countries within the continent are transforming and attracting those who had left to come back. For instance, "Christa Kalulu, for instance, came back recently from eight years in Zimbabwe to run a marketing company. She finds Zambia a changed place, full of opportunities for entrepreneurs" ("Clambering back – Zambia", 2005) and "The growth has drawn back the Ethiopian diaspora, who had fled the famine-prone country. They are returning now with expertise and capital" (Wonacott, 2011).

Industries, industrialization and the diversification of industries are also given agency in the rise of the continent. Roxburgh and Lund (2010) stated,

> Looking ahead, we project that at least four groups of industries on the continent could together generate as much as $2.6 trillion in annual revenue by 2020, or $1 trillion more than today, measured in 2010 dollars. The biggest business opportunity of the four lies in consumer goods and services, followed by natural resources, agriculture, and infrastructure.

This echoes the modernization paradigm of development (Lerner, 1958; Waisbord, 2001) where industries and industrialization played a crucial role in economic growth and development and the "takeoff stage" of Rostow's stages/model for economic growth (Peet & Hartwick, 2015) which represents a period of high growth, as alluded to within the rising discourse. Here, it is important to note that the emphasis of the "takeoff stage" within the modernization paradigm was used to justify foreign intervention through aid, while within neoliberal development and the rising discourse, it is used to justify foreign intervention through trade.

In conclusion, the rising discourse involves and engages multiple social actors each with their own agendas for the continent. While the continent itself is a social actor, other social actors are displayed with much more agency. What makes the rising discourse captivating is how these various social actors are situated within it while also advancing it. While the rising discourse seems to come and go over the past 20 years, the presence of these social actors who have continuously enacted it even during periods when the discourse was "dormant" demonstrates how a discourse can continue to silently work through social actors.

References

Africa rising; The hopeful continent. (2011, December 3). *The Economist*, *401*(8762), 15(US). General OneFile.

Agreement signed for EAC standard gauge railway. (2024, June 7). *Railway PRO*. https://www.railwaypro.com/wp/african-countries-committed-to-sgr-network/

Appadurai, A. (1990). Disjuncture and difference in the global cultural economy 1990. *Cultural Theory: An Anthology, 2011*, 282–295.

Bhorat, H., Kharas, H., & Pita, A. (2017, November 22). Africa's expanding middle class. *Brookings*. https://www.brookings.edu/podcast-episode/africas-expanding-middle-class/

Boumphrey, S., & Brehmer, Z. (2017). *Megatrend analysis: Putting the consumer at the heart of business*.

Childress, S. (2011, January 14). Telecom giants battle for Kenya. *Wall Street Journal*. https://www.wsj.com/articles/SB10001424052748704514504575612012681373530

Castellano, A., Kendall, A., Nikomarov, M., & Swemmer, T. (2015). Brighter Africa. The Growth Potential of the Sub-Saharan Electricity Sector.

Clambering back—Zambia. (2005, June 30). https://www.economist.com/middle-east-and-africa/2005/06/30/clambering-back

Connors, W. (2011, January 18). In Nigeria, used cars are a road to status. *Wall Street Journal.* https://www.wsj.com/articles/SB10001424052748704515904576076622892749928

Deloitte-au-aas-rise-african-middle-class-12.pdf. (2012). https://www.dropbox.com/home/Dissertation/Data/Textual/Reports?preview=deloitte-au-aas-rise-african-middle-class-12.pdf

Doing it my way; Ethiopia and Kenya. (2013, March 2). *The Economist, 406*(8825), 12(US). General OneFile.

Drummond, M. P., Thakoor, V., & Yu, S. (2014). *Africa rising: Harnessing the demographic dividend.* International Monetary Fund.

Emerging Africa. (1997, June 12). *The Economist, 343*(8021), 13-. General OneFile.

EY's attractiveness program Africa 2017. (2017). https://www.ey.com/za/en/issues/business-environment/ey-attractiveness-program-africa-2017

Foster, V., & Briceño-Garmendia, C. M. (2009). *Africa's infrastructure: A time for transformation.* The World Bank.

Francois, J. M., Miriam. (2007). *Institutions, infrastructure, and trade.* The World Bank. https://doi.org/10.1596/1813-9450-4152

Gorecki, I. (2020, September 24). *Kenya's standard gauge railway: The promise and risks of rail megaprojects | Wilson Center.* https://www.wilsoncenter.org/blog-post/kenyas-standard-gauge-railway-the-promise-and-risks-of-rail-megaprojects

Harvey, D. (2007). Neoliberalism as creative destruction. *The ANNALS of the American Academy of Political and Social Science, 610*(1), 21–44. https://doi.org/10.1177/0002716206296780

Joining hands to unlock Africa's potential: A new Indian-industry led approach to Africa | McKinsey. (2014, January 3). https://www.mckinsey.com/featured-insights/india/joining-hands-to-unlock-africas-potential

Kristof, N. (2007, July 5). *Africa: Land of hope—The New York Times.* https://www.nytimes.com/2007/07/05/opinion/05kristof.html

Kristof, N. (2012, June 30). *Africa on the rise—The New York Times.* https://www.nytimes.com/2012/07/01/opinion/sunday/africa-on-the-rise.html

Kristof, N. D. (1997, May 25). Why Africa can thrive like Asia. *The New York Times.* https://www.nytimes.com/1997/05/25/weekinreview/why-africa-can-thrive-like-asia.html

Kulish, N. (2017, December 20). Africans open fuller wallets to the future. *The New York Times.* https://www.nytimes.com/2014/07/21/world/africa/economy-improves-as-middle-class-africans-open-wallets-to-the-future.html

Leke, A., Lund, S., Manyika, J., & Ramaswamy, S. (2014). *Lions go global: Deepening Africa's ties to the United States.*

Lemm, V., & Vatter, M. (2017). *Chapter 4: Michel Foucault's perspective on biopolitics in: Handbook of Biology and Politics* (pp. 40–52). https://www.elgaronline.com/edcollchap/edcoll/9781783476268/9781783476268.00012.xml

Lerner, D. (1958). *The passing of traditional society: Modernizing the Middle East.* http://psycnet.apa.org/psycinfo/1959-08081-000

Manyika, J., Cabral, A., Moodley, L., Moraje, S., Yeboah-Amankwah, S., Chui, M., & Anthonyrajah, J. (2013). *Lions go digital: The Internet's transformative potential in Africa*. McKinsey & Company.

Marsh, J. 2018, October 18. *The Chinese phone giant that beat Apple to Africa*. CNN. Retrieved February 27, 2019, from https://www.cnn.com/2018/10/10/tech/tecno-phones-africa/index.html

Mcgeary, J., & Michaels, M. (1998, March 30). Africa Rising. *Time*, *151*(12), 34–44.

Onishi, N. (2016, January 25). *African economies, and hopes for new Era, are shaken by China—The New York Times*. https://www.nytimes.com/2016/01/26/world/africa/african-economies-and-hopes-for-new-era-are-shaken-by-china.html

Peet, R., & Hartwick, E. (2015). *Theories of development, third edition: Contentions, arguments, alternatives*. Guilford Publications.

Pieterse, J. N. (2009). Representing the rise of the rest as threat Media and global divides. *Global Media and Communication*, *5*(2), 221–237.

Rose, G. (2016). *Visual methodologies: An introduction to researching with visual materials*. sage.

Roxburgh, C., & Lund, S. (2010, August 26). *Booming Africa: An opportunity for Europe | McKinsey*. https://www.mckinsey.com/mgi/overview/in-the-news/booming-africa-an-opportunity-for-europe

Soy, A. (2023, October 13). *China's belt and road initiative: Kenya and a railway to nowhere*. https://www.bbc.com/news/world-africa-67101736

Sun, I. Y., Jayaram, K., & Kassiri, O. (2017). *Dance of the lions and dragons: How are Africa and China engaging, and how will the partnership evolve?* McKinsey.

The lion kings? - A more hopeful continent. (2011, January 6). https://www.economist.com/finance-and-economics/2011/01/06/the-lion-kings

The new champions. (2008, September 20). *The Economist*, *388*(8598), 6(US). General OneFile.

There is hope; Africa. (2008, October 11). *The Economist*, *389*(8601), 20(US). General OneFile.

van Blerk, H., & Mwaura, N. (2018). *African Lions: Who are Africa's rising middle class?* Ipsos. https://www.ipsos.com/en/african-lions-who-are-africas-rising-middle-class

Van Dijk, T. A. (2013). *News as discourse*. Routledge.

Van Leeuwen, T. (2013). The representation of social actors. In Texts and practices (pp. 41–79). Routledge.

Waisbord, S., & others. (2001). Family tree of theories, methodologies and strategies in development communication. *Rockefeller Foundation*, *99*.

Wasserman, H. (2016). Shifting power relations, shifting images. *Africa's Media Image in the 21st Century: From the "Heart of Darkness" to "Africa Rising"*, 193.

Wonacott, P. (2011, January 13). A continent of new consumers beckons; as disposable incomes continue to climb, multinationals shift focus from resources to retail. *The Wall Street Journal Eastern Edition*, B1. General OneFile.

5 Trophy Countries

In as much as the various reports suggest that the entire African continent is rising, a closer look at the reports shows that only certain countries within the continent are identified as rising. This prompts a series of questions. Which countries on the continent are rising and why? Why are the rest of the countries not identified as rising? What are the tensions and contradictions in how the rising countries are selected? What does this reveal about geopolitical interests on the continent? What does this say about the agency of countries to articulate their own value? This chapter addresses these questions, focusing on "trophy countries", that is, the countries listed within previously discussed reports as success stories of the rising discourse.

"Game of Musical Chairs": Dancing to the Tunes of Neoliberalism

As mentioned earlier, the rising discourse has been present for almost 20 years albeit inconsistently, with various institutions producing and circulating their own rising reports at different times. While some of these reports have cited similar countries as rising, there have been instances where the list of countries has varied. This could be because the reports have been produced by different institutions at different times in the past two decades. It is therefore interesting to see which set of countries are the top dogs at a specific time. It is also interesting to see how countries that are considered as rising at one point lose their seat at the table in a different report, with new players coming in, almost making it seem like a game of musical chairs, as countries dance to the tune of neoliberalism. Below is an instance of how these reports identify or project which countries within the continent are rising.

> An analysis by The Economist finds that over the ten years to 2010, no fewer than six of the world's ten fastest-growing economies were in sub-Saharan Africa (see table). The only BRIC country to make

DOI: 10.4324/9781003472124-5

> the top ten was China, in second place behind Angola. The other five African sprinters were Nigeria, Ethiopia, Chad, Mozambique and Rwanda, all with annual growth rates of around 8% or more. During the two decades to 2000 only one African economy (Uganda) made the top ten, against nine from Asia. On IMF forecasts Africa will grab seven of the top ten places over the next five years (our ranking excludes countries with a population of less than 10m as well as Iraq and Afghanistan, which could both rebound strongly in the years ahead.
>
> (*The Lion Kings? – A More Hopeful Continent*, 2011)

From the above excerpt which mirrors various other reports in naming particular countries as rising, it illustrates the problem of a totalizing discourse that suggests that the entire continent is rising, when it is only certain countries in the region. The countries identified as rising by various reports have included South Africa, Nigeria, Ghana, Kenya, Uganda, Botswana, Mozambique, Chad, Benin, Liberia, Mauritius, Rwanda, Lesotho, Zambia, Tanzania, Eritrea, Mali and Senegal (EYs Africa Attractiveness Survey, 2012, 2013, 2017, 2018; "Emerging Africa", 1997; Kristof, 2012, 2007, 1997; Mcgeary & Michaels, 1998; "The lion kings? – A more hopeful continent", 2011; "The gateway to Africa?", 2012; "There is hope; Africa", 2008; "The new champions", 2008). While some countries like South Africa, Kenya, Nigeria and Ghana have been consistently identified as rising, the rise of other countries such as Zambia and Uganda has come into question as will be later discussed, with new players such as Rwanda and Tanzania coming into the picture. But what makes these countries to be identified as the rising stars of the continent and how are they positioned in relation to one another?

Neoliberal Trophies

I refer to the countries identified above as rising as "trophy countries" or "neoliberal trophies", because as a trophy is used to show and mark an accomplishment, these countries are used to show the "success" of neoliberal reform in African countries. Like an athlete holding up their trophy, these countries are raised up, to show other countries within the continent and the rest of the world, the "transformative" effects of neoliberalism. Like a trophy is used to award an accomplishment, these countries represent the work that various institutions such as financial institutions have put into the continent to address its problems.

These countries serve as neoliberal trophies because they were among the first to adopt neoliberal reform. Parading the success stories of these countries is a way of nudging other countries on the continent who haven't gotten on the neoliberal train, to get on. Selecting these countries as the rising ones resembles the diffusion of innovations theory (Rogers & Shoemaker, 1971) where a new idea "innovation" is traced as it spreads in a community or society. As an innovation spreads, those who adopt it quickly are referred to as the "early adopters" with "laggards" being the last to adopt. The countries being heralded as rising can be viewed as the "early adopters" of neoliberal reforms and are used to prompt the "laggards" to join the bandwagon, as illustrated by the excerpt below:

> A second priority for Africa is also a matter of helping Africa to help itself. Africa still receives $15 billion a year in official assistance. It may seem obvious that this should go to the most wretched countries. And yet, paradoxically, there is a case for giving much of it to countries such as Uganda and Cote D'Ivoire, which are leading reform. The reason is the power of local example. Early visible success in those places, as measured by higher growth rates and more foreign investment, will do more than a decade's worth of sermons from the IMF and the World Bank to spur on Africa's laggards.
>
> (Emerging Africa, 1997)

Of course, the excerpt above is problematic in its framing, as it shows how countries who have not adopted neoliberal reforms are othered, by using phrases such as "most wretched countries" and "Africa's laggards". It also shows how countries that have adopted neoliberal reforms become more desirable to Western institutions as shown in the excerpt below.

> How many countries are worth backing in a big way? Mozambique is everyone's favourite example. Recovering from war, it received aid worth half its national income in the mid-1990s. It has grown quickly and become less dependent on aid in recent years, not more. Ghana is usually second on the list. Its economy has grown steadily and its government has also raised more in tax revenue, not less, since the aid started flowing. Others could join the queue – Tanzania, Ethiopia, for instance – with some ifs, buts and wait-and-sees.
>
> (Helping Africa Help Itself – Helping Africa, 2005)

The excerpt above also shows the problem that comes with using the same neoliberal rubric to evaluate the success of countries that each have different socioeconomic, political, cultural and historical backgrounds. While it may seem that these countries are rising at the same pace, these differences affect how well they have been able to meet specific neoliberal conditionalities, influencing their rank on the rising list. It also shows the ephemeral nature of the list of countries identified as rising as the list of countries changes. More importantly, this ephemerality shows how the institutions dictating which countries are rising and which ones are not are forced to grapple with the unevenness of neoliberal reform on the continent. A report by Goldman Sachs reckons with this unevenness of neoliberalism by categorizing the countries within the continent as "Thriving, Driving, Striving and Surviving" (Scott-Gall, 2012). They expound on this stating:

> The first contains South Africa, Gabon and Angola. South Africa stands apart as the most developed African economy, well positioned to benefit from the emergence of the rest of the continent, and with a diverse portfolio of exports, a good infrastructure and mature consumers. Gabon boasts strong oil reserves and is looking to leverage its literate young population to build a stronger services industry in order to diversify its profile. Angola still has to sustainably resolve its political issues, but it has one of the most attractive portfolios of resources (oil, gold, diamonds and copper) which has driven most of its annual double-digit growth over the last decade. The second category contains countries that we expect to be "Driving" Africa's growth potential over the next decade. They enjoy good resources, attractive demographics and an increasing focus on agriculture. But they have to improve their governance, infrastructure and education (among other factors) to be able to improve their per capita GDP. Finally, the "Striving" category contains countries that lag on the development and wealth curve but could be lifted along with the region's broader enrichment, provided that they maintain social stability. The ones left are mostly the big, land-locked countries in the centre that need to be less politically volatile to progress.
>
> (Scott-Gall, 2012, p. 2)

Labeling countries in this way is problematic because it assumes that the conditions in each of the countries are all the same – yet in reality they each have differing socioeconomic and political conditions that influence the success of implementing neoliberal reform. Just as the diffusion of an innovation is mediated by various socioeconomic and political factors in different settings, with different results, the same can be argued about neoliberal reform in various African countries. That is why the countries that have experimented with neoliberal reform have had different results as reflected in the excerpt from the Goldman Sachs report above. The report above also shows the problematic nature of using a neoliberal rubric where the value of the countries listed as rising is based on what they can provide to Western nations.

Similarly, other reports cite different reasons why specific countries they have identified are rising, for instance, the rise of countries such as Mali, Ghana and Senegal are framed in terms of democratic reform, Mozambique, Eritrea, Nigeria and Kenya are framed in terms of privatization. Each country is considered rising because they have been able to successfully implement specific neoliberal terms better than other countries. The rise of each country is articulated differently, as the idea of rising is expressed differently, in different settings and taking on different meanings in different African countries. This is also seen as social media users from various African countries or the diaspora use hashtags such as #GhanaRising, #KenyaRising, #NigeriaRising, etc. to highlight the various ways their countries are doing well. Interestingly, these hashtags draw from the tropes, imagery and metaphors discussed in Chapter 2.

Each country's rise is different, making an overarching "Africa Rising" discourse problematic, as the nuances within each individual rising country are lost. It shows the complexity of neoliberal reform, although prescribed as a panacea for development, it is not a one size fits all, as countries navigate the various conditionalities differently. This complicates the rising discourse as countries engage with the same conditionalities of neoliberalism in different ways, with varying degrees of success. It creates some tensions and contradictions within the discourse as countries with unique profiles are uniformly judged, echoing the quote by Albert Einstein "Everybody is a genius. But if you judge a fish by its ability to climb a tree, it will live its whole life believing that it is stupid". In this same regard, judging countries with different profiles using the same neoliberal conditionalities means some countries won't fair as well as others. This also ends up creating a binary and "othering" within the continent of countries considered rising and those not rising.

"Getting Economic Development Right": Neoliberal Othering Within the Rising Discourse

As discussed previously, representations can include or exclude social actors. The use of trophy countries in the representation of Africa as rising implicitly excludes other countries on the continent, who don't fit neatly within the terms of neoliberalism. In suggesting they are specific countries that are rising and progressing, it also implicitly implies that other countries are not. This leads to "othering" countries within the continent that have been slow to implement neoliberal reforms. It also others countries that might have chosen a different path to economic growth and development. It promotes US-centrism as it privileges neoliberal reform to any other model of economic growth and development.

For example, Ethiopia was listed as one of the countries that had chosen state-led development where "Markets and foreign investors are allowed but mistrusted. The model borrows from China and is conceived as a rejection of Western free-for-all capitalism. It claims to nurture local employers and protect them from Wall Street predators" ("Doing it my way; Ethiopia and Kenya", 2013). In the same report, Ethiopia's state-led model is compared to Kenya's neoliberal economic reform where although there is acknowledgment of growth in Ethiopia, there is skepticism and mistrust toward this growth, questioning whether "it reaches the poor". Meanwhile, Kenya's neoliberal model is reported more positively with no questions. In a different report, Ethiopia and Rwanda which both had state-led development models are recognized as the rising countries on the continent stating, "Some that have begun to get economic development right, such as Rwanda and Ethiopia, have become politically noxious" ("Africa rising; The hopeful continent", 2011). Here, one can see that, although there is some acknowledgment of growth in countries that chose another model for economic growth and development, there is still a lot of skepticism of their approach. This also shows the ambivalence and fleetingness that comes with being identified as rising as these countries still experience socioeconomic and political challenges that are viewed as a threat to their growth.

Apart from comparing countries that are rising to those that are considered not rising or with different economic development models, the rising discourse also others by comparing the trophy countries to each other. Pitting countries against each other is a characteristic of neoliberalism that promotes competition to spur growth. In stating that these are the biggest players, and these others are performing dismally, countries begin to compete for these top spots, as they want to look good not only regionally but also globally. Being listed as one of the rising countries on the continent attracts investment, which is one of the goals of neoliberal reform. This notion of competition is alluded to in relation to South Africa:

> It did indeed once serve as a landing slot for investors wary of venturing into shakier African countries to the north. But in the past couple of decades the continent as a whole has become a lot more peaceful, democratic and stable. As a result, investment has been pouring in – and often bypassing South Africa. Some African countries, with economies growing twice as fast, are challenging its claim to be the region's obvious first stop for investors. The economy of Nigeria, with some 158m people to South Africa's 50m, has been roaring along at an annual rate of almost 7% for the past eight years – and may even become Africa's biggest by 2016, with Egypt (82m people) hot on its heels. At the same time, Ghana and Kenya, among others,

> are competing with South Africa to host the African headquarters of foreign multinationals.
>
> ("The gateway to Africa?" 2012)

Similarly, other reports also draw comparisons between the rising countries on the continent stating:

> Size matters here. Benin is nicely democratic – it has more political parties than cities – but with a mere 9m people it carries little weight. Nigeria, on the other hand, has 160m, so along with Kenya and South Africa it sets the tone in regional meetings and institutions – and it still struggles to get things right.
>
> ("Bye-bye Big Men – Côte d'Ivoire, Ghana and Nigeria", 2013)

The above excerpt also shows how countries with different profiles as previously discussed are compared against each other. The irony is that these countries that are different from one another are expected to rise in the same way, a contradiction within the rising discourse. This is further demonstrated here, "The transformation of Lagos is worth trumpeting. Its economy is now bigger than the whole of Kenya's" ("Bye-bye Big Men – Côte d'Ivoire, Ghana and Nigeria", 2013). The irony here is that a city in Nigeria (Lagos) is compared to a country (Kenya), without mentioning the geopolitical differences between Nigeria and Kenya. A reader with no geographical reference might assume that these are two countries on the continent, not a city and a country. Even with geographical reference, this comparison fails to take into account the geopolitical differences within the continent. What these excerpts ironically show is that while various countries have been awarded rising status, they are positioned alongside each other to compete with who is rising more. This comparison is also problematic because it reinforces the idea of Africa as homogenous.

When it tries to show the heterogeneity within the continent, it is still pitting countries against one another as shown in this quote that alludes to Eritrea's difference from other African countries. It suggests a level of superiority because it does not have a lot of the other problems that some African countries have. "This is not Africa; people will tell you in Eritrea. What they mean is that the country is astonishingly free of the social plagues that taint much of the continent. There is no tribalism or sectarian division here" (Mcgeary & Michaels, 1998). This quote also shows how much some Africans have internalized the pessimistic representations of other countries within the continent that deem them as better. It shows the nuanced way Africans view their countries in relation to other countries on the continent. It also shows how Africans position their countries between the pessimistic and rising discourses. It shows that there is othering within the continent, a consequence of the rising discourse. These comparisons within the continent are also a way of reinforcing national identity, as people take pride in the growth of their countries, evidenced through social media and Afrocentric digital platforms with hashtags such as #Ghanarising, #Ethiopiarising, etc. These comparisons of growth also extend outside the continent, with rising African countries being compared to other rising nations.

"32 Times Greater": The Rise of Asian Countries Versus African Countries

The comparison between rising countries is not just within the continent, it extends to countries in Asia that have been identified as rising. China, South Korea, Singapore and India are some of the countries with growing economies that have been compared to rising African countries. Through these comparisons, the progress of African countries is set against the rise of Asian countries, whose economies flourished and grew faster than African countries. Even though the rise of African countries is being celebrated, comparing it to Asian economies suggests a failure of African countries to embrace neoliberalism soon enough and catapult their economies. Focusing on the Democratic Republic of Congo, the author below compares its economic growth to South Korea, arguing that the two countries were at the same income level in the 1950s. Although they allude to "cultural and historical advantages" that may have influenced South Korea's growth, those are quickly dismissed by the implicit assumption that replicating neoliberalism would be the panacea for African economies.

> The area around this river port city in eastern Congo, the former Zaire, is a case in point: it is dilapidated and impoverished yet studded with diamonds, like a billionaire on Skid Row. Back in the 1950's, when this country and several others in Africa were at the same income level as South Korea while blessed with far more natural resources, it might have seemed reasonable that Africa would soon leave Asia in the dust. A wave of new research into the contrast between Africa and East Asia is producing some surprising findings. The most striking and reassuring conclusion is that although East Asia enjoyed some significant cultural and historical advantages, its economic boom relied on factors that probably can be replicated elsewhere.
>
> (Kristof, 1997)

South Korea's growth has also been compared to that of Ghana ("There is hope; Africa", 2008) and Zambia ("Clambering back – Zambia", 2005). Both of these comparisons cite how South Korea has grown over 30 times more than Ghana and Zambia, even though all of these countries were at the same level in the 1950s. The reports also fail to acknowledge that Ghana, Zambia and other African countries were still under colonization in the 1950s. Comparing them to other countries in the world gives a false sense of reality since they were not even socioeconomically and politically free. The two reports also heavily rely on the pessimistic discourse citing a history of disaster, to reinforce the idea that Asian economies have grown significantly more than African economies. This further reinforces the idea that the pessimistic and rising discourses heavily rely on each other to be meaningful.

"The lion kings? – A more hopeful continent" (2011) argues that the average income of Africans was about four times that of China in 1980 with China three times richer in 2011.

This problematic comparison not only homogenizes Africa but once again the argument that African countries should be doing better. The irony here is when institutions were relying solely on the pessimistic discourse to talk about Africa, the idea that African countries were seemingly doing better or could do better was inconceivable.

The comparison to rising Asian countries also shows how the discourse of the "Rise of the rest" has pitfalls where othering takes place, between the rising countries. It is also interesting that the rise of African countries seems to be reported more regionally as the rise of Africa, while the rise of countries such as China and India are discussed more as national entities, even though there are instances where they are discussed regionally. For instance, Botswana was cited as the fastest-growing country worldwide ahead of South Korea, Singapore and China (Kristof, 2007); the tendency is to use Botswana to represent Africa yet the aforementioned Asian countries stand alone. Additionally, the othering between African countries and the Asian countries is used to justify neoliberalism as the ideal path to development for African countries and other countries in the Global South.

"This African Success Story Is Turning Sour": From Sweethearts to Jilted Lovers

A challenge of the Africa Rising discourse as pointed out earlier is in how ephemeral its terms are. The terms of neoliberalism demanded certain conditions from African countries such as democratize their politics, privatize institutions, get rid of corruption, etc. These conditions became hard to attain for countries, and as donors came to that realization, they began to punish countries for not attaining them. Countries that were previously heralded for their rise because of adopting neoliberal reform began to struggle and quickly lost their rising status. In other words, the rising status depended on how well countries succeeded in adopting neoliberal reform. Countries previously considered as darlings or sweethearts of Western donors soon became jilted lovers. It is also interesting how interests shift from countries on the continent, depending on how well they play ball with US donors. Uganda is one such country as shown by the excerpt below.

> So much of the credit for the change since then must go to Yoweri Museveni, who has been president since 1986. But progress under his rule has relied heavily on western donors' largesse. Indeed, in the 1990s, Mr. Museveni became a pin-up of international aid givers, who cited Uganda as an example of how aid really could transform a country. Now, however, doubts are growing as to whether Uganda really has turned a corner or whether it is not slipping back into a familiar pattern of big-man politics and corruption.
>
> ("Down, down, up, and maybe down – Uganda", 2005)

The above excerpt shows how conditionalities such as the need for governments to adopt democracy were not always met or met as well as US donors thought they would be. Because of that, countries such as Uganda which adopted some of the conditionalities successfully and struggled with others such as democracy had their rising status reconsidered. Other rising countries such as Nigeria and South Africa also experienced the same.

> Since the start of this year, the outlook across the continent has grown grimmer, especially in its two biggest economies, Nigeria and South Africa. Their currencies fell to record lows this month as China, Africa's biggest trading partner, announced that imports from Africa plummeted nearly 40 percent in 2015. "We can see what drove the growth in Africa when demand goes away", said Greg Mills, the director of the Brenthurst Foundation, a Johannesburg-based economic research group. "Well, demand has gone away, and it's not pretty." The International Monetary Fund has in recent months sharply cut its projections for the continent. Credit rating agencies have downgraded or lowered their outlook on commodity exporters like Angola, Ghana, Mozambique and Zambia, which were the darlings of international investors until just over a year ago.
>
> (Onishi, 2016)

In yet another report:

> Some ambled through the decade rather than sprinted. Africa's biggest economy by far, South Africa, is one of its laggards: it posted average annual growth of only 3.5% over the past decade. Indeed, it may be overtaken in size by Nigeria within ten to 15 years if Nigeria's bold banking reforms are extended to the power and the oil industries
>
> ("The lion kings? – A more hopeful continent", 2011)

These excerpts show how countries that were once considered the rising stars of the continent are losing their allure and show the challenges of neoliberal reforms on the continent as countries which are unable to adhere to the prescribed terms and begin to lose their status. This also once again shows how discourses influence how people and institutions think and act. When countries adhered to the terms of neoliberalism, they were the darlings/sweethearts of investors; however, once they began not meeting some of the terms, they became jilted lovers. This is further illustrated by these two reports in the same issue of *The Economist*, "Down, down, up, and maybe down – Uganda", 2005 and "*Clambering back – Zambia*" (2005) which compare the progress in these two countries with Uganda once a rising sweetheart being jilted for Zambia.

> Yet that stability is at risk because of Mr Museveni's desire to stay in power. Once viewed by most donors as a progressive leader, he is using parliament to amend his own constitution of 1995 that limited presidents to two terms in office; his second expires in less than a year. This week, malleable MPs voted for a constitutional amendment to let him seek re-election. So donors are feeling queasy. Ambassadors are warning Mr Museveni and his governing circle of the dangers of putting personal interests above national ones. To mollify the donors, Mr Museveni will hold a referendum at the end of this month on whether to allow a return to multi-party politics. But many fear that allowing a bit of pluralism may be just a trade-off for letting Mr. Museveni become president for life. Earlier this summer, Britain symbolically cut [pounds sterling] 5m ($9m) of aid in protest against Mr. Museveni's ambition to stay on; Ireland may follow suit.
>
> ("Down, down, up, and maybe down – Uganda", 2005)

In comparison Zambia during the same period was considered the new "bae" by donors. They began shifting their attention from Uganda to Zambia.

> The donors still like Mwanawasa enough.... Mr Mwanawasa was elected with just 29% of the vote and is probably no more popular

> now than he was in 2001. His cabinet, well stocked with cronies and relations, has only a couple of good ministers, it is said, and he shows no enthusiasm for the constitutional reform for which many Zambians currently clamor. Yet he receives high marks from "the donors" – the ambassadors and other foreign officials whose views may persuade the G8's leaders to open, or keep closed, their pocketbooks at Gleneagles next week.
>
> (Clambering Back-Zambia, 2005)

Here, it is interesting to see how quickly the rising status shifts across the continent. While it may seem like a good thing that more countries are considered rising, it is not. This is because the terms under which rising countries are chosen depend on US donors and how well countries follow their conditions. This also shows the problem with the conditions set by US donors, because they created an all-or-nothing mentality that set countries up for failure. If you did not do well in one area but did well in another, it did not matter. This is why China's approach without all the conditionalities set by US donors became very attractive to African governments.

Apart from these shifts where previously rising countries begin to fall, in other instances, countries that had been deemed hopeless begin to be considered as rising. For instance, Sierra Leone which was the focus of "The Hopeless Continent" edition of *The Economist*, in the year 2000, stating:

> Indeed, since the difficulties of helping Sierra Leone seemed so intractable, and since Sierra Leone seemed to epitomise so much of the rest of Africa, it began to look as though the world might just give up on the entire continent... In itself, Sierra Leone is of no great importance. If it makes any demands on the world's attention, beyond the simple one of sympathy for its people, it is as a symbol for Africa.
>
> (The Hopeless Continent, 2000)

Interestingly in 2011, *The Economist* caught the "Africa Rising" fever and did its first rising edition identifying Angola, Equatorial Guinea, Zimbabwe, Ethiopia, Rwanda, South Africa and Mauritius as the rising countries. Africa was no longer "*The Hopeless Continent*". In 2013, they did a second "Africa Rising" edition where Sierra Leone which was previously condemned was labeled one of the rising countries stating:

> Sierra Leone has seen a full decade of peace after an 11-year civil war that killed 50,000 people. Development is slow and most people remain poor. Rice is imported from Thailand at great expense

> because, despite fertile soil and plenty of rain, its own agriculture is too inefficient to produce enough. But at least violence has become rare. On average, fewer than a hundred people out of 7m are murdered in a year, according to official statistics – a fifth of the rate in New York. Private guns have been banned. Less than a decade after welcoming the world's largest and perhaps most successful UN peacekeeping force, which collected many of the guns, Sierra Leone is secure enough to send blue-helmeted troops on a similar mission to Sudan.
>
> (Tired of War – Guinea-Bissau, Guinea and Sierra Leone, 2013)

Once again, here one can see how the notion of rising is articulated in relation to the ceasing of violence in Sierra Leone, Guinea and Guinea Bissau, with Sudan now labeled as a country that is not rising due to the existing unrest. Ironically, in the year 2000 "The Hopeless Continent" edition of *The Economist*, Mozambique and Ethiopia were labeled as hopeless cases when *Time* in their "Africa Rising" edition in 1998 had identified them as rising. One of the contradictions within the rising discourse is how, when and which countries different institutions identify as rising. The list of rising countries changes depending on who is speaking and when they are speaking. One is left wondering who is really rising and who isn't. Another contradiction here is that while this is about the rise of African countries, the decision on who is rising is from outside the continent.

In conclusion, this chapter shows how problematic it is to fit all the countries on the continent within the pessimistic discourse or the rising discourse. Looking at the specific countries identified as rising begins to reveal the nuances within this discourse. It also reveals the complexity of the rising discourse and how deeply intertwined it is with the neoliberal agenda set by international financial organizations for African countries. Additionally, it also shows that they are shifts not only between the pessimistic and rising discourses but also within the rising discourse itself. It also shows how these reports by various institutions by naming some countries as rising and others as not rising, not only influence how these countries are perceived globally but also influence the flow of resources to these countries. It influences how African countries and Africans view themselves in relation to one another, establishing a binary between the rising countries and the so-called "laggards". It demonstrates how power is exercised within the rising discourse as various institutions have the power to decide which countries are rising and which ones are not. While this discourse has been celebrated as a breath of fresh air after centuries of Afro-pessimism, it begs the question of whether it is an alternative discourse or just another instance of "the west" exercising power over "the rest", in this case African countries.

References

Africa rising; The hopeful continent. (2011, December 3). The Economist, 401(8762), 15(US). General OneFile.

Clambering back—Zambia. (2005, June 30). https://www.economist.com/middle-east-and-africa/2005/06/30/clambering-back

Doing it my way; Ethiopia and Kenya. (2013, March 2). The Economist, 406(8825), 12(US). General OneFile.

Down, down, up, and maybe down—Uganda. (2005, June 30). https://www.economist.com/middle-east-and-africa/2005/06/30/down-down-up-and-maybe-down

Emerging Africa. (1997, June 12). https://www.economist.com/leaders/1997/06/12/emerging-africa

EY's Africa attractiveness survey. (2012). Retrieved March 6, 2019, from https://www.ey.com/za/en/issues/business-

EY's Africa Attractiveness Survey 2013. (2013). Getting down to Business, 76.

EY's attractiveness program Africa 2017. (2017). https://www.ey.com/za/en/issues/business-environment/ey-attractiveness-program-africa-2017

EY's attractiveness program Africa 2018. (2018). https://www.ey.com/za/en/issues/business-environment/ey-attractiveness-program-africa-2018

Helping Africa help itself—Helping Africa. (2005, June 30). https://www.economist.com/leaders/2005/06/30/helping-africa-help-itself

Kristof, N. (1997, May 25). Why Africa Can Thrive Like Asia. *The New York Times*. https://www.nytimes.com/1997/05/25/weekinreview/why-africa-can-thrive-like-asia.html

Kristof, N. (2007, July 5). *Africa: Land of hope—The New York Times*. https://www.nytimes.com/2007/07/05/opinion/05kristof.html

Kristof, N. (2012, June 30). *Africa on the Rise—The New York Times*. https://www.nytimes.com/2012/07/01/opinion/sunday/africa-on-the-rise.html

Mcgeary, J., & Michaels, M. (1998, March 30). Africa Rising. *Time*, *151*(12), 34-. General OneFile.

Onishi, N. (2016, January 25). *African economies, and hopes for new era, are shaken by China—The New York Times*. https://www.nytimes.com/2016/01/26/world/africa/african-economies-and-hopes-for-new-era-are-shaken-by-china.html

Rogers, E. M., & Shoemaker, F. F. (1971). Communication of Innovations; A Cross-Cultural Approach. http://eric.ed.gov/?id=ED065999

Scott-Gall, H. (2012). *Africas Turn* (No. 27; Fortnightly Thoughts). Goldman Sachs.

The gateway to Africa? South Africa. (2012, June 2). *The Economist*, *403*(8787), 62(US). General OneFile.

The hopeless continent | May 13th 2000. (n.d.). *The Economist*. Retrieved August 31, 2024, from https://www.economist.com/weeklyedition/2000-05-13

The new champions. (2008, September 20). The Economist, 388(8598), 6(US). General OneFile.

The lion kings? - A more hopeful continent. (2011, January 6). https://www.economist.com/finance-and-economics/2011/01/06/the-lion-kings

There is hope; Africa. (2008, October 11). The Economist, 389(8601), 20(US). General OneFile.

Tired of war—Guinea-Bissau, Guinea and Sierra Leone. (2013, March 2). https://www.economist.com/special-report/2013/03/02/tired-of-war

6 Conclusion

Africa Rising or the Rise of Neoliberalism in Africa?

The representation of African countries in global media has always been contentious due to the problematic ways that these representations essentialize and disempower these countries. But what about representation that seemingly casts a positive light on the continent? What are the consequences of such a representation? This book has examined the construction of the African continent as "rising", analyzing the ways this representation is embedded in global power structures that continue to influence the dynamics between African countries and the rest of the world. While the dominant pessimistic discourse has been interrogated by various scholars, a critical analysis of the rising discourse was lacking. In conducting a critical discourse analysis of various texts produced by various social actors, which include media institutions, international financial, development and business organizations, this dissertation reveals how the rising discourse is immersed in a complex web of global power relations. In other words, it is not just a celebratory discourse about the continent, rather its emergence reveals the influence of global power relations exercised over the continent. These global power dynamics are made apparent in these temporary shifts between an Afro-pessimistic discourse to Africa Rising. While the Africa Rising is not a consistent discourse, like the dominant pessimism, these intervals between the two discourses make the rising discourse much more visible, and it is within these intervals that global power dynamics are revealed.

First, global power dynamics are revealed through these intervals between the two discourses as they reflect a shift in development discourses, where modernization, dependency and participation were articulated more in relation to Afro-pessimism, while Africa Rising is articulated more in relation to neoliberal development and globalization. This is not to say that neoliberal development completely supplants earlier paradigms of development, rather, by looking at these intervals between the pessimistic and rising discourse, these shifts in development discourse are clearer.

DOI: 10.4324/9781003472124-6

Secondly, in relation to development, the intervals between the rising and pessimistic discourses also reveal the connections between the modernization, dependency, participatory and neoliberal globalization. The connection between modernization and neoliberalism can be seen in how various reports reference the role of industrialization as a means to development. The connection between neoliberalism and dependency is reflected in how neoliberalism is framed as a solution to the reliance on economic aid, with countries finally being able to rely on the markets. The connection with the participatory approach is in neoliberalism promoting democracy and allowing for "everyone" to be able to participate in the economic growth of their countries. Neoliberalism is tasked with solving the challenges that other paradigms of development could not. These earlier paradigms set the stage for neoliberalism, and this is most visible within the shift in discourses from pessimism to rising. It is also within these shifts in discourse and the intervals between them that you see the influence and involvement of BRIC countries as they "partner" with African countries, with these partnerships becoming a means to economic growth and development. Again, the failures of neoliberal reform set the tone for China's partnerships with African countries.

Thirdly, it is within these shifts in discourse from pessimism to rising and the intervals that occur between them that the complexity of the rising discourse is revealed first through its connection to the pessimistic discourse. As previously discussed, the rising discourse is heavily associated with the dominant pessimistic discourse. Afro-pessimism is used to justify the rising discourse. By declaring that the continent is rising, the pessimistic discourse becomes more significant, as it is used to illustrate that things were bad and now, they are getting better. Relying on the pessimistic discourse makes it easy to explain the rise of the continent away. The shift between the two discourses is also reflected in how the tropes, metaphors and languages used to talk about pessimism are transformed through neoliberalism to become "new" symbols within the rising discourse, for instance, women and children have been used to represent pessimism, but they become symbols of the rise of the continent after neoliberalism. As such, the rising discourse is informed by the pessimistic discourse.

Fourth, these shifts in discourse also show how various social actors think and act toward the continent. While the pessimistic discourse was to warn the world of the perilous conditions in African countries, and why outsiders should stay away from it, the rising discourse is to attract the rest of the world to have an interest in African countries, because of all the opportunities they now present. While the pessimistic discourse was to dissuade investors, the rising discourse persuades them that African countries are the next global frontier. As discussed in Chapter 5, the rising discourse influences the movement of the various scapes (Appadurai, 1990) as a new scramble for the African continent develops. Within these shifts you also see how the role of existing social actors such as governments and international development organizations changes as they become technologies used to advance neoliberalism. You also see the emergence of new social actors within the civil society such as non-profit organizations, private entities such as multinational firms, countries such as those considered rising within the continent and other countries in the Global South, media networks including Afrocentric digital platforms with new regional and global networks of power being formed. These shifts reveal how power is allocated and exercised as illustrated in Chapter 4 that discusses the various social actors within the rising discourse.

Fifth, it is within these shifts that entail the redefinition of the roles of various social actors, emergence of new social actors, redefinition of old and emergence of new regional and global power networks that you see neoliberal globalization at its best in African countries. It is here that the "transformative" power of neoliberalism is made more clear, with the neoliberal "successes" of the continent put on a pedestal and used to justify why other countries should get on board.

Sixth, these shifts also influence the contours of Africanity, that is, the relations between African countries, as "neoliberal trophies" emerge, and these countries are viewed as the powerhouses of the continent while other countries are considered to be lagging behind. This also influences the movement of scapes within the continent, as these countries become regional power centers within the continent, setting the tone for the rest of the continent, with scapes such as mediascapes moving from these centers to the rest of the continent and the world. This is illustrated through Afrocentric digital platforms that are having a growing influence on how African countries, cultures and identities are perceived both within and outside the continent, as they present a more nuanced understanding. This shift in discourses and the notion of Africanity is also demonstrated in how Afropolitans are having agency in telling their own versions and engaging with the rising discourse as discussed in Chapter 3. What this also demonstrates is how nuanced and complex the rising discourse is in itself with some agreeing with it by redefining what it means for Africa to rise by creating other tropes such as culture as a symbol of Africa's rise.

Finally, it is also within these shifts in discourse and the intervals between them that you also see the contradictions and absences embedded in the rising discourse.

Contradictions and Absences

One of the contradictions of the rising discourse is how it continues to essentialize the continent. As illustrated in Chapter 5 on trophy countries, only specific countries within the continent are considered as rising. However, this discourse still labels the entire continent as rising just as with the pessimistic discourse. Not only does this discourse essentialize the continent, but it also essentializes neoliberalism as the only form of economic reform that can work on the continent. This is in the way it dismisses countries that have not adopted neoliberal reform or not fully complied with the conditions of neoliberalism, as not rising.

Another contradiction within this discourse, especially in Anglo-American media institutions, the rise of African countries is taken with a grain of salt, as they express cautious optimism in how long this trend of growth will last or use the uneven growth of some countries as a problem with those countries as opposed to, perhaps, a problem with neoliberal economic reform. Here, neoliberalism is treated as a one size fits all, and indeed, African countries with their own dynamic profiles show the problem of this approach, as different countries display different degrees of success or failure with neoliberal reform. As discussed in Chapter 5, governments in African countries are social actors within the rising discourse; however, to what extent do these governments and their leaders have agency within the structure of neoliberalism? The rubric used to decide which countries on the continent are rising also shows where the agency lies in terms of deciding which African countries as rising. Anglo-American media institutions and international financial, development and business organizations exercise their agency in declaring that the continent is rising and naming the countries they consider as rising. While this may be fantastic for countries considered rising (Chapter 6), it indicates an imperialist gaze on the continent, as African countries seem to be rising on somebody else's terms. It also reflects hegemony as African countries are governed by outside forces and internally as governments turn their citizens into neoliberal subjects. While it may seem by looking at the rising discourse that Africans don't seem to have much agency, if any, Afrocentric digital platforms can be seen as Africans exerting their own agency within neoliberal structures, by using these platforms to express other ways that African countries, cultures and identities are rising, or even to contest the rising discourse. Even within these platforms however, contradictions exist because while some editors and contributors don't agree with the rising discourse or see it as just another extreme discourse, some of the stories they tell within these platforms to challenge the negative perceptions about the continent draw on the tropes of the rising discourse such as entrepreneurship, innovation and democracy. This demonstrates what Harvey (2007) asserts:

> Neoliberalism has, in short, become hegemonic as a mode of discourse and has pervasive effects on ways of thought and political-economic

> practices to the point where it has become incorporated into the commonsense way we interpret, live in, and understand the world.
>
> (p.23)

Additionally, as noted in Chapter 4, the middle class is one of the tropes of the rising discourse. In Chapter 3 we see that even within the Afrocentric platform, it is the African middle class who seem to be invested most in the representations of the continent, as they have access to the resources that allow them to participate digitally. The middle class thus also becomes agents of the rising discourse. One can thus see how neoliberalism has become so ingrained in the psyche, such that it is unconsciously reproduced within these platforms and other institutions.

A discourse is not only about what it includes but also what it excludes. As such, what does the rising discourse exclude? The rising discourse especially from Anglo-American institutions is very invested in highlighting neoliberal economic reform, in doing so, it however excludes any other country within the continent that may be approaching economic reform differently. Such countries are excluded from the rising discourse as if they have nothing to offer until they implement neoliberal reform. The rising discourse also dictates the specific standards by which a country can be considered rising. As discussed in Chapter 5, this leads to othering countries on the continent that do not adhere to these standards as misfits. To be more inclusive of other countries on the continent, perhaps, the rising discourse needs to be more than just neoliberal conditionalities, something that Afrocentric digital platforms begin to capture as they show other ways that African people, cultures and identities are succeeding. Although, even within Afrocentric digital platforms, not all African countries are included, this, they argue, is not intentional, rather, due to challenges such as language barriers, connectivity and press freedom in some countries, although the desire is there.

In conclusion, the Africa Rising discourse offers a lens to examine the ways in which globalization processes are unfolding within Africa. It also shows who are the major social actors influencing globalization on the continent. It also shows how globalization is affecting countries on the continent similarly and differently. It also shows the roles that digitaltechnology and social media platforms have in influencing the perception of Africa in the global imaginary.

References

Appadurai, A. (1990). Disjuncture and difference in the global cultural economy 1990. *Cultural Theory: An Anthology*, *2011*, 282–295.

Harvey, D. (2007). Neoliberalism as Creative Destruction. The ANNALS of the American Academy of Political and Social Science, 610(1), 21–44. https://doi.org/10.1177/0002716206296780

Index

For Product Safety Concerns and Information please contact our EU representative GPSR@taylorandfrancis.com
Taylor & Francis Verlag GmbH, Kaufingerstraße 24, 80331 München, Germany

www.ingramcontent.com/pod-product-compliance
Lightning Source LLC
LaVergne TN
LVHW010939110826
845149LV00013B/2672

* 9 7 8 1 0 3 2 7 5 0 4 4 6 *